PENGUIN BOOKS

ELIZABETH BOWEN

Patricia Craig is co-author (with Mary Cadogan) of three critical studies, including *The Lady Investigates: Women Detectives and Spies in Fiction* (1981). She is a freelance critic and regular contributor to *The Times Literary Supplement* and the *London Review of Books*. She was born and grew up in Belfast and now lives in London.

LIVES OF MODERN WOMEN

General Editor: Emma Tennant

Lives of Modern Women is a series of short biographical portraits by distinguished writers of women whose ideas, struggles and creative talents have made a significant contribution to the way we think and live now.

It is hoped that both the fascination of comparing the aims, ideals, set-backs and achievements of those who confronted and contributed to a world in transition and the high quality of writing and insight will encourage the reader to delve further into the lives and work of some of this century's most extraordinary and necessary women.

Patricia Craig

Elizabeth Bowen

Penguin Books

Penguin Books Ltd, Harmondsworth, Middlesex, England
Viking Penguin Inc., 40 West 23rd Street, New York, New York 10010, U.S.A.
Penguin Books Australia Ltd, Ringwood, Victoria, Australia
Penguin Books Canada Limited, 2801 John Street, Markham, Ontario, Canada L3R 1B4
Penguin Books (N.Z.) Ltd, 182–190 Wairau Road, Auckland 10, New Zealand

First published 1986

Made and printed in Great Britain by
Richard Clay (The Chaucer Press) Ltd,
Bungay, Suffolk
Set in Monophoto Photina

CONTENTS

Henry Cole Bowen (photo: Audrey Fiennes)

Florence Bowen (photo: Audrey Fiennes)

Elizabeth learning not to be a muff. Her mother and an old family groom are looking on (photo: Audrey Fiennes)

Elizabeth as a young woman in the dining room at Bowen's Court (photo: Finlay Colley)

Same period: the writer at work (photo: Finlay Colley)

1938: Elizabeth drawn by Mervyn Peake (photo: Mary Evans Picture Library)

The Camerons snapped at Bowen's Court (photo: Finlay Colley)

In the library at Bowen's Court, 1947: a gathering of friends. Jim Gates is standing in the middle (photo: Finlay Colley)

Bowen's Court (photo: The Irish Architectural Archive, Dublin)

Elizabeth regarding some odd-looking pieces of sculpture in the grounds at Bowen's Court. (She called them 'the Uglies') (photo: Finlay Colley)

2, Clarence Terrace, Regent's Park: the Camerons' London home, photographed in 1945 (photo: National Monuments Record)

Alan Cameron lighting a cigarette (photo: Finlay Colley)

On the back of this snapshot Elizabeth has written: 'Cat with kittens – me and some of the "creative writing" students at Seattle (University of Washington). The brunette beside me, wearing the white rose, is a little hellcat: she wrote *the* most *brilliant* story!' (photo: Finlay Colley)

1957: Elizabeth with some Kildorerry neighbours (photo: BBC Hulton Picture Library)

1970: At a christening party for the Connollys' son. Elizabeth in conversation with Cyril Connolly, Joy Craig and Caroline Blackwood (photo: Deirdre Levi)

A formal portrait by Cecil Beaton (photo: Sotheby's London)

7 June, 1899	Elizabeth Bowen born at Herbert Place, Dublin.
1907	Settles with her mother in England.
1912	Death of her mother. Moves to Harpenden, Hertfordshire to live with her aunt.
1914	Enters Downe House School, Kent, as a boarder.
1919	Spends two terms at school of art in London.
1923	*Encounters* published. Marries Alan Cameron and moves to Northamptonshire.
1925	Moves to Old Headington, Oxford.
1927	*Ann Lee's* published.
1928	*The Hotel* published.
1929	*The Last September* published. *Joining Charles* published. Becomes well known in literary circles in London and Oxford.
1930	Inherits Bowen's Court, Co. Cork, on the death of her father.
1930–9	Many house parties at Bowen's Court. Reviews for periodicals such as *New Statesman*, *Spectator*, *Tatler*.
1931	*Friends and Relations* published.

1932	*To The North* published.
1934	*The Cat Jumps* published.
1935	*The House in Paris* published.
	Moves to Clarence Terrace, Regent's Park, London, on Alan Cameron's appointment to the BBC.
1937	Member of the Irish Academy of Letters.
1938	*Death of the Heart* published.
1939	Becomes an air-raid warden.
1940	Employed by Ministry of Information to carry out warwork in Dublin. Travels frequently between London, Dublin and Co. Cork. In London during blitz.
1941	*Look at All Those Roses* published. Meets Charles Ritchie.
1942	*Bowen's Court* published.
	Seven Winters published.
	English Novelists published.
1944	Clarence Terrace damaged by V2 bomb.
1945	*The Demon Lover* published.
1946	'Castle Anna' produced at Lyric, Hammersmith.
1946 on	Broadcasting for BBC.
1948	Companion of the British Empire.
1948–50	Acting principal at Kent Education Committee's summer school for teachers of English at Folkestone. Lecture tours for British Council.
1949	*The Heat of the Day* published.
	Appointed to the Royal Commission on Capital Punishment. Honorary Doctorate from Trinity College, Dublin.
1950	*Collected Impressions* published.
1951	*The Shelbourne* published.
	Moves to Bowen's Court.
1952	Death of Alan Cameron.

PREFACE

Elizabeth Bowen, Anglo-Irishwoman, novelist, inheritor of an ancestral home, but no accompanying income, literary hostess, party-giver, stayer-on in London during the war, wife of a BBC official, lover of a diplomat, observer of people's foibles, acute evoker of atmospheres, sardonic social commentator, distinguished woman of letters and indefatigable worker, was born in 1899 and died in 1973. She grew up along with the twentieth century, and took careful note of all its vagaries and upheavals. Her novels and stories put her at the forefront of modern writers; and she conducted her life with stylishness and integrity.

In preparing this short biographical study I have been greatly indebted to Victoria Glendinning's *Elizabeth Bowen: Portrait of a Writer* (1977). Other main sources of reference are: *The Siren Years: Undiplomatic Diaries 1937–45* by Charles Ritchie (1974); *Elizabeth Bowen: An Estimation* by Hermione Lee (1981); Virginia Woolf's Letters and Diaries; Elizabeth Bowen's letters to Virginia Woolf, in the possession of Sussex University, and to William Plomer, in the possession of Durham University. The information about Elizabeth Bowen's wartime activities in Dublin comes largely from Robert Fisk's *In Time of War* (1983).

I am grateful to everyone who helped with suggestions or recollections, and especially to Emma Tennant, for her unfailing kindness and encouragement, to Tony Lacey at Penguin, and to Jeffrey Morgan, for constant moral support. Thanks are also due to Audrey Fiennes, Finlay Colley and Noreen Butler for their help in providing photographs.

ONE

In *The Little Girls* (1964) a child comes out with an announcement about a dead sheep in a wood, a remark occasioned by Elizabeth Bowen's own recollection of a dead sheep, though one in rather nastier shape. The real sheep, hit by a train, remained at the back of the author's mind for more than fifty years, to be called up when some such image was needed. Within a day or two, the real-life corpse had vanished from the embankment where it lay; but, the author says, 'that was far from the last of it'. It had become an infinitesimal item in the novelist's stock of material.

The cleaned-up corpse in the novel provides a very small instance of the way things are altered for fictional purposes. In this novel, too, although none of the three little girls of the title is a self-portrait, the one who comes closest to it, Diana (Dicey) Piggott, lives with her mother in a seaside villa, just as Elizabeth Bowen did: Southstone in the novel, Folkestone in reality. Between 1907 and 1912, Florence Bowen and her daughter inhabited a succession of villas in Kentish coastal resorts, and inland: Folkestone, Lyminge, Seabrook and Hythe.

What took this Irish pair to the south of England, where the architecture was a far cry indeed from the austerity of Georgian Dublin? There's a family misfortune at the bottom of their departure: the breakdown and voluntary confinement in a mental hospital of Elizabeth's father Henry Cole Bowen. An idyllic period in the little girl's life was thereby brought to an end. The novelist has left an enchanting record of her earliest years – the part of them, at any rate, that was spent in the city. The title of this short exercise in autobiography is *Seven Winters* (1942). Summers belonged to Co. Cork, where the family home, Bowen's Court, was located. Each spring, Elizabeth and her mother would board the Mallow train at Kingsbridge station, returning to Dublin in October. 15 Herbert Place was the Bowens' Dublin address – a Georgian house of light brown brick, with high front steps, facing a canal. Each year, on their return from Cork, the canal would be clotted with fallen leaves.

It was at Herbert Place, on 7 June 1899, that Elizabeth Bowen was born – 'the only June I spent in Dublin until the summer when I was twenty-one'. Her parents had been married for nine years, and she – who surprised them by being a daughter, when they'd expected a son – was their only child. (To their credit, she says, 'they did not once murmur at my being a girl'.) No previous Bowen generation had lacked a son to inherit Bowen's Court, one of those Irish 'big houses' in which the idea of an ascendancy was embodied.

Both the idea and the building programme flourished towards the end of the eighteenth century. Things were rather different at the start. 'We north-east County Cork gentry began rather roughly, as settlers . . .', Elizabeth wrote in her family history *Bowen's Court* (1942). The first Bowen settler (from the Gower Peninsula) came over with Cromwell, and acquired the Farahy lands, near the Bally-houra Mountains, of an Irish Catholic gentleman named Garrett Cushin. Perhaps this dispossessed Irishman refused to move far from his confiscated property, and became a nuisance to the Welsh usurper; for Colonel Bowen made it a condition of his son's inheritance that no marriage should take place between him, John Bowen, and Eilis Cushin, 'or any of Garrett Cooshin's ffammyly'.

Colonel Bowen needn't have worried; his descendants, on the whole, preferred heiresses for their brides. It was the money imported into the family by Jane Cole, who married the Cromwellian soldier's great-grandson in 1716, that went to the making of Bowen's Court ('first Bowen house on the first Bowen's land'). The house was built by Jane Cole's son, another Henry Bowen, and completed in 1775 – the heyday of 'the Protestant nation'. By this time, the settler mentality had given way to a self-confidence, throughout the whole ascendancy class, and a flair for elaborate living. Social privilege, in Ireland, was confined to this class, 'ignorance and barbarism' being the condition in which the bulk of the population was supposed to be sunk. (It wasn't until 1928, with the publication of Daniel Corkery's *The Hidden Ireland*, that the resilience of Gaelic Munster received full acknowledgement.) The old, disaffected Irish, by and large, looked back to an idyllic Gaelic past – however imaginary – while the newcomers looked forward to social position and prosperity. The 'mere Irish' – 'mere' having become a term of disparagement, though it had started simply by meaning 'true' – viewed the imposed aristocracy with disfavour in which a certain amount of derision was included. (A famous instance of this is the petition addressed by the Munster poet, Eoghan O Rathaille, not to one of the Gaelic Mac-Carthys, his family's traditional overlords, but to an English incomer with the preposterous name of Valentine Brown: the name comes in for a lot of ironic repetition.) Rapparee activity – with the original victims of land confiscation, like Garrett Cushin, bent on making life a misery for their supplanters – petered out, but there was plenty of sporadic harrying of property owners to take its place. Oath-bound organizations, like the Whiteboys and Right Boys, which flourished for a time in Co. Cork, as elsewhere, had their own way of obtaining redress for agrarian ills. One of their practices was to immerse an offender, in the dead of night, in a pit of water filled with briars.

The single native gesture of hostility towards Bowen's Court didn't amount to very much. In 1798, in the aftermath of the United Irish uprising, some local insurgents converged on the house, but were driven off by its (fore-warned) inhabitants. There were some casualties among the attacking party – the leader, for one, hastily buried in his elegant boots, and a man left behind in the spot where he died: up a pear tree at the front of the house. 'So,' Elizabeth wrote, 'the tip, and the very poor shoddy tip, of '98 touched Bowen's Court.' A piffling instance of reckless and disorganized behaviour it must have seemed, indeed, to the people of the great house.

None of the Bowens, neither Elizabeth nor any of her

ancestors, seems to have been at all captivated by the glamour of the burning injustice or the lost cause; in common with many of their class, the Bowens of the eighteenth and nineteenth centuries held themselves aloof from radical aspirations or seditious murmurs, concentrating their attention on family life, cultivating a keen sociability, marrying their cousins, and seeing to the running of an estate. (They also went in for litigation, not always with happy results; one of them gambled away the side of a mountain; and some were unrestrained spenders.) The condition of the country impinged on such people only when it reached an apex of wretchedness. The year known as Black '47 came; in a corner of Farahy churchyard a famine pit was dug, and from the basement of Bowen's Court soup was dispensed – feverishly, and not to much purpose. Eliza Wade, a Bowen widow and Elizabeth's great-grandmother, threw herself into the effort to stave off starvation for a few: but the nearby famine pit was soon chock-full. The bodies of those too weak to make the soup-kitchen lay strewn along the approach to Bowen's Court.

Elizabeth's grandfather Robert, the last of the 'high-voltage' Bowens, as she put it, was at school in Cheltenham during the Famine. He went on, in due course, to marry, to redecorate the house in quintessential Victorian style – satin-striped, beetle-green curtains, satin upholstered couches, sumptuous carpets, gilt everywhere – and to set himself at loggerheads with his eldest son, Elizabeth's father. Between father and son a temperamental incompatibility prevailed. One, the elder, was practical and overbearing, the other intellectual, well-mannered and vague. Henry Bowen, born in 1862, was the first of thirteen children, of whom nine survived. They grew up animated, whole-hearted and rather highly-strung. From the story 'The Happy Autumn Fields', in the wartime collection *The Demon Lover*, you gain an inkling of the pleasures, routines and alliances available to such a family. The story amounts to an imaginative reconstruction of life at Bowen's Court, one generation before Elizabeth's. The comings and goings of boys at boarding school, dramas with locked trunks, family outings, mysterious affinities, the congestion and isolation (as Elizabeth has it) of the big house ... All this had dwindled, within thirty years or thereabouts, to a solitary child – Elizabeth – occupying the nursery and schoolroom, and that only for half the year. But she was no less socially-minded than her predecessors.

Her sociability was, in part, an inheritance from her mother's family, the Colleys of Mount Temple, Clontarf – a large Victorian house overlooking Dublin Bay. Florence Colley, who came third in a family of ten brothers and sisters, and was rather more wayward than the others, married Henry Bowen in 1890. The Colleys, with their unimpeachable family history and connections – nothing untoward there, no obsessiveness or inbreeding or rackety inclinations – were of slightly more consequence, in the social sense, than the more complicated Bowens. Elizabeth, in *Bowen's Court*, does her best to make her Colley grandmother seem likeable; but there is really too much of the Victorian matriarch about the old lady for her to bring it off. Confident, clever and anti-intellectual (as Elizabeth says), Mrs Colley was also very particular when it came to deciding

whom to admit to her Dublin home. She drew the line at
solicitors and brewers, though a barrister or a wine mer-
chant might get in. Fortunately Henry Bowen, when he
came in pursuit of Florence, had been called to the Bar.
(After Trinity he had opted for a profession, greatly to the
chagrin of his father Robert, who would have it that the
administering of an estate was sufficient occupation for the
heir to Bowen's Court. Robert must also have seen Henry's
attitude as a betrayal, especially after the weakening of the
position of landowners, as he would see it, by Gladstone's
Act of 1881, which allowed the tenant greater freedom.
Henry would almost certainly have found himself disinherited if the property hadn't been entailed. As it was, a
lot of bad feeling was engendered between father and son,
which persisted until Robert's death in 1888.)

Florence Colley, one generation away from the Victorian
hauteur we detect in her mother, seems to have been
endowed with gumption, as well as inventiveness and
charm; there was also a strain of vagueness in her nature
which matched her husband's. Their daughter saw in their
relationship a kind of innocence and nobility that wasn't
susceptible of alteration. Things going badly wrong, as they
did, didn't damage the regard each had for the other.

We can't help feeling that Henry and Florence Bowen,
who lived in Dublin throughout the nineties, carried
vagueness a bit too far in relation to the literary revival
which was going on under their noses. They never noticed
it. 'Anglo-Ireland,' their daughter explained, still 'looked for
culture everywhere but inside her home shores.' The people
she had in mind certainly wouldn't have expected to come

upon culture in the dingy classrooms tenanted by the Gaelic League. The vitality and verbosity of the remote west, as envisaged by Synge (himself a Protestant Anglo-Irishman), they would have found unattractively alien. Yeats, who would end by equating the whole ascendancy class with grandeur and integrity, was still in thrall to ancient Ireland. Were the Bowens ever among the audience at the Irish Literary Theatre or its successor, the Abbey? Their daughter thinks not: the Gaiety would have been more to their taste. Not that Henry, at least, was ever a devoted theatre-goer: the cinema, once it became available as entertainment, appealed to him more.

A jig was danced on the kitchen table at Bowen's Court to celebrate the birth of Elizabeth; six weeks later, she, her mother and her nurse, 'drove down the upper Avenue in an inside car'. The last of the Bowen's Court Bowens had arrived at her ancestral home. Years later, remembering the summers that followed, she mentions white muslin, the dresses of little Anglo-Irish girls clustered together in pews for the Sunday morning service at Farahy church, and an India-muslin dress of her mother's with a green-stained hem: it 'was always trailing over the grass' – and, incidentally, epitomizing Edwardian picturesqueness. Tea – the weather during these childhood summers being characteristically fine – was taken out of doors, in a corner of the big tennis lawn. She remembered the phaeton in which her great-grandmother Eliza Wade (the famine-fighter) used to bowl through the grounds in her old age (it must have been regarded as an antique by the early 1900s); parties; social visits; governesses; fancy hats. She took an interest, when she was old enough to do so, in the other solitary little girl who'd lived at Bowen's Court: Miss Prittie ('Miss Pretty'), niece of the house, who had made a hyacinth garden there in a clearing near a wood in the 1790s. What became of Miss Pretty? No one knew; only a rumour said she had died young.

At Herbert Place, from October to May, a constant friendly hum could be heard from a saw-mill across the water of the canal; nearby were mysterious streets, with possibly something sinister at the end. Elizabeth, whom a contemporary taught to stand on her head, wasn't taught to read before the age of seven, as her mother didn't want her to strain her brain. Florence, who had definite ideas about bringing up children, saw to it that her daughter drank sufficient milk (the alternative being to grow up runty and bandy-legged), wore gloves as a precaution against freckles (a Bowen defect, along with the tendency to queer the brain), and eschewed shyness: 'she detested children who "burrowed" when they were introduced'. Shyness was common, and dull to boot: good manners mattered, among the Anglo-Irish.

Elizabeth (called 'Bitha' during this period, as she couldn't get her tongue round 'Elizabeth') grew familiar with a rather imposing Dublin – Sackville Street ('the widest street in the world'), Trinity College, the eighteenth-century Bank of Ireland at College Green, the Four Courts. On Sunday afternoons, before her Colley grandmother died in 1904 and the family scattered, she and her parents would visit Mount Temple, going by tram to Clontarf, and getting off at a corner where the smell of evergreens 'mingled with a stagnant smell of the sea'. She would likely have worn a scarlet cloth coat – as did the capering child in 'The Inherited Clock', whose 'mother had got [her] up in a perfectly sickening little scarlet coat, like a monkey wears on a barrelorgan' – and a tam o' shanter, with a white muff on a white silk cord hung round her neck. The terraced lawns, the big double drawing-room, and the banter of her uncles and aunts were all a source of pleasure to her. The stretch of mudflats called the Bull she associated with Europa, having been introduced to mythology early, and not having the least idea that Clontarf is a simple transliteration of the Irish phrase *Cluain Tarbh*, the plain of the bull.

One thing that struck her about the Dublin she inhabited was the fact that every front door was furnished with a brass plate proclaiming the occupier's business: a sensible device, it seemed to her. Professional people had moved into these splendid houses when the old nobility moved out after the Union, but Elizabeth wasn't aware of any comedown about the matter. Of any house not bearing the informative plaque she took a distinctly scornful view.

Dancing was one of the social skills she was supposed to acquire; and so, to a class at the Molesworth Hall she set out once a week, very well wrapped up against the Dublin chill ('In those days, everybody subscribed to the idea that children were perishable'). Once inside the building, she would suffer the layers of clothing to be removed by her governess, until she stood there, in company with many other little girls and a boy or two, in the requisite white muslin dress. Neither this, nor the many parties she had to attend, seem to have aroused the slightest apprehension in her; she wasn't afflicted with a dread of social occasions ('I pity people who do not care for Society,' she later wrote). She didn't like pulling crackers: that was all. Once, having marched off to a party wearing a dress her mother had criticized, she suddenly glimpsed herself in a mirror while eating a strawberry ice-cream, and understood the point of her mother's objections. It put her off ice-cream for years.

Children's parties, expeditions to the famous shops in Grafton Street, feeding the ducks on the lake at Stephen's Green: these were part of a well-regulated childhood that allowed no access to the untoward. The other Dublin – seedy, raucous, threatening or merely ramshackle – remained unknown, as far as Elizabeth was concerned. No tenement-dwellers, barefoot and bare-faced, ever jeered at her in her smart reefer coat. She knew, however, of poverty-rotted houses where the walls might crumble at any moment, and experienced a slight *frisson* at the thought of such places.

Protestant, professional Dublin, though she didn't know it at the time, was set apart from the rest of the city, through being immune to disaffection and disquiet; its character was founded on an idea of privilege and propriety, tempered with social expertise. It refused to have truck with swank or fuss. It went in for moderation and tolerance in all its doings (taking care not to expose itself too readily to the intolerable) and believed in calling things by their proper names: Church of Ireland, not Protestant Church, Roman Catholic, not Catholic. It spoke properly too. It's difficult to understand how the bulk of the Anglo-Irish managed to live in Ireland without acquiring an Irish intonation: but they did. 'To

25

speak with a brogue, in my childhood,' Elizabeth wrote, 'was to be underbred.'

Elizabeth didn't know any Roman Catholics (except, possibly, some children at her dancing class), and wasn't curious about them; the whole business of religious difference – like differences of sex and class – had something faintly embarrassing about it. It was an area into which she didn't wish to intrude. When she came to look back, she was very funny about certain Catholic practices – a 'predisposition to frequent prayer,' she remarked, 'bespoke, to me, some incontinence of the soul.' It wasn't, of course, until many years later that she became conscious of any ambivalence in the position of the Anglo-Irish; in the early part of her childhood she'd have considered the whole race well-established and justly fortunate. No one told her of the revolt that was taking place against English images of the Irish, or of the parallel drive to reinstate Irish distinctiveness. It wouldn't have behoved her family to take an interest in the *Playboy of the Western World* ructions, Maud Gonne acting her heart out as Cathleen Ni Houlihan, St Enda's school founded on true Fenian principles, and all the rest of it. They'd have been affronted by the very fierce nationalism of two Northern Protestant poets, Alice Milligan and Ethna Carberry, who hotly envisaged some forms of revenge for bygone 'Saxon' atrocities. As it was, word of the Irish revival didn't get through to Elizabeth until 1916, when she was at school in England.

When she was five, a little girl called Gerry Bridgeford ('mad on horses') whose parents were in India, came to stay with the Bowens for a year. It was during this year that

Henry Bowen's mental illness began. He became un-characteristically irritable, and allowed unreasonable self-reproach and worry to get a grip on him. Anxieties, past and present, loomed larger in his mind than they need have done. He had left the Bar for the Land Commission, and the new working pattern didn't altogether suit him. Florence's apprehensions about the Bowen tendency to overwork hadn't been ill-founded. She, however – Elizabeth says – was probably the last to notice anything seriously amiss; a courteous detachment would have kept her from questioning Henry's odder behaviour. But it wasn't long before the true state of affairs was apparent even to Florence.

Henry was in the throes of a nervous breakdown ('an-aemia of the brain' was the diagnosis). For most of the summer of 1905 Florence stayed with him at Herbert Place, still hoping he would conquer his illness. Elizabeth and Gerry Bridgeford, meanwhile, were at Bowen's Court, in the charge of a rather emotional English governess who referred to the pair of them as 'the babes'. She read 'Perseus' to them and encouraged them to sing 'Twinkle, Twinkle' when visitors came. 'I am SO SORRY about Mr Bowen,' this governess wrote to Florence, around whom friends and relations were rallying in Dublin. ('She loved my mother embarrassingly,' says Lois of a past governess in *The Last September*.) When Henry went to England for treatment, the management of the Bowen finances and other practical matters fell to the lot of Florence, who wasn't equipped to handle them. Her husband's brother, and her own brother, had to step in more than once.

The treatment didn't do Henry very much good. Back at

Herbert Place, with his wife and daughter, during the winter of 1905–6, he became increasingly distraught. Elizabeth, however, 'did not notice much'; the resolutely imperturbable attitude of relatives like her Uncle George and Aunt Laura Colley helped in this respect. (Many years later, in a letter to Virginia Woolf, Elizabeth mentions a Colley cousin, 'very homesick', whom she's looking after in London: 'His father was very good to my mother when my father was ill. This is more than thirty years ago but one has to work out that sort of understanding kindness from one generation to another, like the inverse of a vendetta.') Was this the start of what she later called 'a career of withstood emotion'? It wasn't to be expected that the grown-up crisis should leave the child unscathed; but, she says, she came out of it with nothing more disabling than a stammer.

Florence, having been advised to leave Henry for a time, took Elizabeth across to England, where most of her Colley relatives had settled after the sale of the Mount Temple house. They stayed first with Elizabeth's Fiennes cousins at Ealing (Audrey Fiennes, child of Florence's sister Gertrude, was to remain one of Elizabeth's closest friends all her life), and then went on a series of visits. It wasn't until late in the summer of 1906 that they managed to put in some weeks at Bowen's Court. Here, by a new Welsh governess, Elizabeth was finally taught to read. She was seven, and not absolutely enthralled by the prospect of literacy. Being read to was a treat she'd always relished. In the event, she became an avid reader – one of 'the heady ones', as she put it, the fiction addicts. (Dickens, E. Nesbit, Baroness Orczy, all intoxicated her.) Was it laziness that kept her from protesting about the late start? She hadn't been deprived of fiction, it's true – still, she hardly seems like a child who'd have tolerated falling behind her contemporaries in the acquisition of any ordinary skill.

That winter, a last attempt was made by Florence to retrieve the family harmony disrupted by Henry's illness; but it didn't come to anything. Henry, Elizabeth explained when she came to write *Bowen's Court*, needed to be alone to fight his demons. One night, 'after a day of alarms' (unspecified), she was taken from her bed in the nursery at Herbert Place, bundled into a cab and deposited on the doorstep of relatives at Killiney. It was the end of a whole section of her life. Florence quickly joined her, and arrangements were made for mother and daughter to set up home in England. There were plenty of forceful relatives to take them in hand. At Folkestone, for example, lived Cousin Isobel Trench (an Archbishop's daughter-in-law) and her family; and so, at Folkestone, the villa life began. The Kent coast, all architectural frivolities – white fretwork balconies, porches, bow windows, ornamental stucco – charmed Elizabeth and, to a lesser extent, Florence. It was the novelty of all the seaside decoration and brightness that went to their heads.

England was represented to seven-year-old Elizabeth as an adventure; she wasn't to be allowed to brood over the circumstances of the flight from Ireland, or the unhappy months preceding it. Ireland had made its mark – if you begin there, she said, Ireland remains the norm, 'like it or not'. England enabled her to savour to the full (in Louis MacNeice's phrase) the drunkenness of things being various.

Georgian Ireland and Edwardian Folkestone were, ex-hilaratingly, at opposite poles. She must have pleased and reassured her mother by showing herself to be unusually sturdy and resilient. The good early upbringing, abundant in care and attention, was paying off. Elizabeth had plenty to fascinate her in the new, slightly off-beat life she found herself leading. (What was made of Florence, we might wonder, 'suspiciously lovely looking', unaccountably single, and not very securely installed in any of the villas that took her fancy for a time? It must have required all her relatives' respectability to counter an impression of flightiness in Florence's proceedings.) For one thing, she acquired a strong sense of history; and history-as-pageant, moreover, not tainted with desolation and unease as it tends to be in Anglo-Ireland. It isn't, for the Anglo-Irish, a subject to dwell on: too inglorious, and too much to reprehend. The triumphant and colourful side of English history, by contrast, proved irresistible to the clever, spirited eight-year-old.

So – the family crisis didn't make Elizabeth especially difficult or highly-strung, her Bowen heredity notwith-standing. However, her good morale wasn't obtained without a measure of repression. Her 'not noticing' was to an extent deliberate; she simply and expediently cut out what she couldn't bear to feel. A refusal to suffer (or at least to suffer unduly), she came to think, is perhaps a characteristic of all children. But events can affect them adversely at some level none the less. Two things, Elizabeth acknowledged much later, apropos of Sheridan Le Fanu's *Uncle Silas*, are terrible in childhood: helplessness, and the feeling that something is being kept from you because it is too bad to be told. She knew what she was talking about. First, an edited version of her father's condition was presented to her – it was always that he was ill, never that he'd gone mad and become impossible to live with. Then, there must have been another conspiracy of evasion on the subject of her mother; we don't know how much Elizabeth was told, or when it became clear to her that Florence (stricken with cancer) was going to die. Her mother's operations were called 'rest cures'. Henry had no sooner recovered (for he fought the illness, and in the end he did recover) than Florence got worse. In the last of the balmy Kentish villas – all archways and inglenooks, and with a garden full of syringa – Elizabeth recorded laconically (as if to be more expansive would admit insupportable feeling), 'she died'.

TWO

Florence Bowen died in 1912, when Elizabeth was thirteen.
Mother and daughter had lived out of Ireland for more than
five years, the move setting up, for Elizabeth, 'a cleft between
my heredity and my environment'. The former, she added,
remained the more powerful. But it was England, she
thought, that made her a novelist, by making her conscious,
and appreciative, of diversity. She looked well at everything
around her: gabled houses, striped awnings, deck-chairs,
sea-fronts, zigzag paths, marshy stretches, sugarmouse
shops, mysterious thickets, the parasols of holiday-makers,
a heat haze over the Leas. It was all taken in.

After the abandonment of the Dublin house, some Bowen
furniture was shipped across to England and then shifted
around Kent. It went 'to Hythe . . . to a villa called Oak
Bank . . . to Erin Cottage at Lyminge, then back to Hythe
again'. Elizabeth, in all these places, asserted her Irishness
by singing affecting ballads like 'The Harp that Once',
though she took a poor view of some Celtophile cousins
who strode about Folkestone looking like Deirdre of the
Sorrows. She wasn't, she says, a disagreeable child, and we

believe her; in any case, there were plenty of relatives to point out blemishes in her character, such as bumptiousness, and agitate for their suppression. Florence, Elizabeth conceded dryly, 'did everything that she could'. Some years earlier, she'd broken it to Elizabeth that she needn't expect to grow up pretty: a nice character would have to do her. (As far as we can judge from photographs, she *was* pretty at two or thereabouts, but became rather plain – abundant, wavy fair hair notwithstanding – before turning out rather handsome. From her mid-twenties on, she could be said to exemplify, as she herself said about one of her ancestors, 'the bony stylishness of [her] race and type'.)

She was never disagreeable, but she could be trying, especially when a showing-off fit was on her. She mentions bragging, bossing and exaggerating among her less attractive temporary traits. Like everyone else, she had bouts of being unpleasant: sulking and so on. Aunts reported an increase in uproariousness when Elizabeth was around. She kept everyone going – this tendency had a bad side as well as a good one. We see her as a vivid, bold, inventive little girl, never stuck for an idea or a retort (though her stammer may have hindered her in getting the latter out). School was good for her, but Florence – with Bowen instability always at the forefront of her mind – periodically withdrew Elizabeth from Lindum, the Folkestone day-school where she'd been enrolled. To give her brain a rest, an easier regime was tried for a time: lessons with a vicar's daughters, the little Salmons, and their caustic governess. Elizabeth, who missed the rough-and-tumble of school life, didn't get on especially well in this situation. Possibly the glowing family life of the Salmons made her feel at a loss – at any rate, she had to assert herself, and did so in typical only-child ways (or so the governess said). After the rectory interlude, she returned, with a measure of relief all round, one imagines, to the 'notice-boards, hockey sticks, creaky desks, smelly inkpots, white mice stowed away in the cloakroom . . .' – all contributing to an atmosphere of commotion which she seemed cut out for, at the time.

Unaccommodating Elizabeth might have been, but she never made herself unpopular; she had too much verve and openness for that. The Salmon girls, she recalls with some surprise, 'felt an affection' for her, for all her bombast; and so did nearly everyone else. She had a talent for friendship. At three, she'd been taken to England to meet her Fiennes cousins for the first time, and three years later they came to Bowen's Court. From then on, wherever Florence and Elizabeth were, Audrey Fiennes stayed with them twice a year, the two girls picking up their friendship where they'd left it off. They invented complicated games, often with a literary basis. Florence, so careful of Elizabeth in some respects, wasn't at all careful in others; she didn't prohibit dicey childhood activities such as bathing off unsafe beaches, headlong horse-riding, or roller-skating round a rink at crazy speed. One of her early dreads for Elizabeth was that the child should grow up a muff.

Florence's free-and-easy attitude enabled Elizabeth and her companions, whoever they chanced to be, to have a hilarious time, enjoying switchback-riding (when they had the money) and all the rest of it. (Only bicycling was forbidden by Florence: that came later.) Elizabeth, as a child, seems to have been rather less sedate, if no less bookish, than the children in her books – though she records their doings, like her own, in that amiably sardonic tone which characterizes her literary manner. She was active and out-going, and not inhibited about expressing affection, par-ticularly for her mother. Did she go as far as 'Darlingest', as the schoolgirl Rosalind does in the story, 'Coming Home'? Probably she did, but only in a play-acting way, with which Florence would have gone along. She is always, in her writ-ing, remarking on the habit of self-parody, which comes easily to the droll. Overblown embraces and endearments, however soundly based, would have struck this fastidious Anglo-Irish duo as irresistibly funny.

Rosalind, in that early story, runs through a whole gamut of emotions – anger, apprehension, remorse – when her mother ('Darlingest') unaccountably isn't at home to greet her on her return from school, bearing exciting news about an essay. She must be dead, the volatile child decides; and when it turns out that Darlingest isn't, it's only a reprieve, not a permanent boon. 'Anything might happen, there was no security.' So Elizabeth might have felt, at a low moment. Or even: 'Life's nothing but waiting for awfulness to happen and thinking about something else.' She needed all the hardihood she was endowed with, to survive the second blow to her happy childhood.

Henry's six-year illness had nearly run its course. By 1911 he was practising again in Dublin – having convalesced at Bowen's Court – and had visited Hythe, where Elizabeth introduced him to her friend-from-next-door, a little girl called Hilary, with whom she was writing a novel about

Bonnie Prince Charlie. (He took the pair of them out to tea: no doubt they'd have worn the ubiquitous white muslin and broad-brimmed straw boaters of the period, and behaved excitedly.) There were cricket matches in season, and sponge cake and ices in shady, inland cafés. Henry and Florence resumed their companionship easily, and a lot of talk took place concerning a return to Dublin. Was it just a show for Elizabeth's benefit? The grown-ups must have understood that no such move would be possible.

Florence had only a year left. In the early summer of 1912 the Bowens, all three, were at Bowen's Court, where Elizabeth was delighted to find everything the same, Miss Pretty's garden included. 'On my thirteenth birthday I woke up early and ran barefoot all over the house . . . The air was fresh with mosses and woods and lawns.' A Colley uncle and his family came to stay. Things seemed almost normal . . . Then, on a wet day in July, Florence left for a Dublin nursing home. By August she was back in Hythe, in an exalted state by all accounts, and very ill. In September, she died.

It was the third Colley death that year. One of Florence's sisters had already died of consumption, and her youngest brother, like Cousin Roland's friend in *The Little Girls*, had gone down on the *Titanic*. The remaining family marshalled its resources: there were things to be seen to. Aunt Gertrude Fiennes broke the news to Elizabeth, who'd been sent to stay next door with Hilary. We remember the trepidation with which Roger, in 'The Visitor', waits for someone to come and tell him that his mother is dead. 'Yes, they had been great companions, always together.' For some time afterwards, Elizabeth was in a state of shock. Shock made her act boisterously on the day of her mother's funeral. Florence soon became a subject, in Elizabeth's mind, about which neither she nor anyone else was suffered to speak. If she cried in the night – as she did – it wasn't to be alluded to.

'At mid-term,' she writes in *Pictures and Conversations*, referring to the autumn term of 1912, 'I entered Harpenden Hall ... still in a state of shock.' At Harpenden, in Hertfordshire, lived an unmarried Colley sister: Aunt Laura, who kept house for her brother Wingfield, curate-in-charge at St John's Church. Florence had arranged for her sister Laura to take charge of Elizabeth, and this is what happened, though quite a few other relatives had a hand in her subsequent unbringing. ('Pauline, an orphan, had been controlled for the last five years by a committee of relatives ...': so we read of a minor character in *To The North*.) Henry returned to his practice in Dublin, but came to Harpenden for the holidays. His grief-filled daughter wasn't disposed to respond to anything, or anyone. She was torn, at this terrible time, between wanting to solicit sympathy, and wanting to repel it. No one could get their manner towards her right – only her Uncle Wingfield, with his shyness and thoughtfulness, came close to it.

In *The Death of the Heart*, Elizabeth Bowen imagines the young girl Portia and her mother Irene trailing up and down the Riviera: until the mother goes into a nursing home, and dies. Did she have the zigzag path at Folkestone in mind when she sent the two of them, mother and daughter, 'arm-in-arm in the dark, up the steep zigzag, pressing each other's elbows, hearing the night rain sough down through the pines . . .'? Portia, we know, winds up in a household somewhat deficient in natural feeling (though those on whom she's foisted do their best). Elizabeth, perhaps, was luckier with the Harpenden semi-detached villa of her aunt and uncle, even if the enormity of her bereavement made the house seem sometimes congested.

Aunt Laura bought her a bicycle – 'a glittering, brand-new Raleigh', on which, winging over the nearby common, she experienced acute exhilaration – and pulled strings to get her into Harpenden Hall, as a day pupil. (Actually, Elizabeth said, she'd have been happier boarding: better no home life at all than a makeshift, inferior kind.) She wore a black tie going to school, by her own choice – a last gesture of remembrance towards her mother. The regulation tie was brown, to match the brown tunic, box-pleated into a square yoke, under which went a blue and white striped blouse. Angela Brazil territory. Like all those cliff-top and manor-house schools in books, the schools attended by Elizabeth had been built for a different purpose (which pleased her). They started as private houses, and underwent conversion which left their wood panelling and Morris wallpapers intact. (Morris wallpapers duly reappear in her fictional schools, Mellyfield, St Agatha's and the rest of them.) At all three schools, learning was, properly, at a premium. You weren't there to idle around.

A certain amount of knowledge was absorbed but not regurgitated by Elizabeth during her Harpenden period: the clever Lindum pupil (she says) had become a veritable dunce. We can put it down to private stress. She had, in any case, another string to her bow, having become the prime mover in various school crazes. (She was never behindhand in putting forward her ideas.) Secret passages, for example, were suddenly the thing – at Elizabeth's instigation. A lot of poking about in cellars ensued. (' "There may be a secret spring," faltered Cicely': so wrote Angela Brazil.) A fashion for the occult followed, and then a phase of enthusiasm for coloured celluloid birds ('stuck tail-down into the rims of our knitted caps'). The box-burying episode at the centre of *The Little Girls* had its origin at Harpenden Hall, though nothing very significant went into the real-life coffer – no superfluous digits or anything of that sort.

In the summer of 1913 Elizabeth travelled abroad with her father and uncle and aunt: Brussels, Cologne and Switzerland. She still wasn't in a mood to be impressed by anything. Her provokingness, she insists, had nothing to do with her age – fourteen; it was rather a case of 'protracted childishness'. Looking back, she is very dry and scornful about the supposed afflictions of adolescence: 'Tormenting, nameless disturbances, conflicts, cravings, were not experienced by me. I had never heard of them.'

So – it was one thing to be moody, quite another to be moony. *That* smacks of a kind of silliness alien to the robustness and decorum conferred on Elizabeth by her upbringing and temperament. Among her endowments, as we have seen, was a fair amount of Anglo-Irish reserve. At some level, as she'd have seen it, it was vulgar to be overcome, by feelings of any kind. You had to keep a hold on moderation and self-mockery.

When she says she never had adolescence at all badly, does she mean that she wasn't struck by sex at an

39

inappropriate age ('... only little commonalities ... had affairs while still at school': so declares a minor character in *The Last September*)? Did the topic arouse in her an impatience dictated by fastidiousness? 'We were not highly sexed,' she said of herself and her contemporaries at Downe House, her third school, making, one feels, a point about the general run of English middle-class schoolgirls at that period. In common with most other people, she was sufficiently intrigued by the facts of life to consult an encyclopedia on the subject. But we can't feel this was a prurient or hysterical act: just a quest for information. In *The Last September*, Elizabeth is derisive about what she calls 'the life force' and those enthralled by it; however, all kinds of social behaviour she noted carefully, with a view to mockery.

Travelling in Europe, that last summer before the war, she was in on the end of an era, though she had no means of knowing it, and wouldn't, at that age, have been elegiacally inclined, in any case. 'Who did kill that Australian Duke?' asks slapdash Dicey – a few years younger than Elizabeth at the time – in *The Little Girls*. Her better-informed classmate is outraged. ' "Austrian," she enunciated, "Archduke. Get that into your head." ' Elizabeth, nearly as unknowing, was at Bowen's Court, preoccupied with a party and with the making of furniture for a dolls' house (both activities shared by her cousin Audrey Fiennes) when news of the war reached Co. Cork. 'All I could say was: "Then can't we go to the garden party?" ' Go she did – to remember Mitchelstown Castle garden, on that momentous day, with a wind blowing down from the Galtee Mountains, and all the assembled loyalists of the south untroubled by the slightest doubt as to where their allegiance lay. 'Not a family had not put out, like Bowen's Court, its generations of military brothers – tablets in Protestant churches recorded deaths in remote battles; swords hung in halls.' The mood in the country at large was, and remained, incomprehensible to the unembittered gentry.

Downe House School, in Kent, had been in existence for only seven years when Elizabeth went there as a boarder in September 1914, but already its standing was high; Elizabeth had been told it was a very good school, and took this, correctly, to mean that it subscribed to a sense of the fitness of things. It was accommodated, at the time, in Charles Darwin's old house near the village of Downe: more Morris wallpaper and white woodwork. Its grounds contained an ilex on a mound and an old mulberry tree, beneath which confidences and recriminations were exchanged. Pupils wore green djibbahs and, outdoors, coats of purple tweed. A sound grasp of facts and a high moral tone were among the ends Downe House had in mind for its girls. As far as the second was concerned, the war was a help: 'We ... could not fall short in character without recollecting that men were dying for us.'

The urbane tone of that observation is an effect of the retrospective view. (Elizabeth's essay on her schooldays, 'The Mulberry Tree', was written in 1935.) So is the humorous insouciance frequently displayed by Elizabeth: on the girls' not taking an avid attitude to men, for example, she blithely comments: 'Possibly the whole sex had gloomy associations.' But even at the time, we gather, Downe House dissociated itself from the patriotic ardour that prevailed elsewhere (and got itself reproduced in girls' stories – and others – of the period). No senior simply longs to drive an ambulance near the lines, and we hear nothing at all about knitting for the troops. Not that patriotism wasn't enjoined on Downe House girls; they were simply required to be level-headed about the matter. It wasn't, for example, the thing to overeat, after the *Daily Mail* had cast aspersions on food-hogs.

You could indulge the silliness peculiar to the school-age group, as long as you were knowing about it. While Elizabeth was there, for instance, a fad for teddy bears (long before Sebastian Flyte) and other stuffed toys hit the school, but this was perfectly all right provided it was an affectation, not an aberration. The headmistress frowned on girlishness, and had an ironic manner which rubbed off on her pupils. It was here, Elizabeth says, that she learned how not to write ('though I still do not always write as I should'). She also learned how to acquit herself well in conversation; meal-times were given over to making good talkers of the girls. You were kicked by the head of your table if you sat there mute. No one, however backward by nature, got away with effacing herself for long. 'Many of us,' Elizabeth observed, 'have grown up to be good hostesses.'

It was in 1916 that Elizabeth belatedly got wind of the Irish literary revival, with its evocations of a Dublin not entirely familiar to her (shabbier and shadier than the one she knew), and learned of the strong impulse, on the part of certain of the Anglo-Irish, to throw in their lot with Irish nationalism – or at any rate, cultural nationalism. But her kind largely remained indifferent to all that, though they would have asserted that their brand of Irishness was as valid as any other. A three-hundred-year association with the country entitled them to feel proprietary about it. That they went on sounding English was a matter of little importance. Neither did you have to rollick to prove your race. Elizabeth, at school, would probably have gone out of her way to confound any ideas the readers of unintellectual novels might have gathered about the madcap Irish.

Henry Bowen, soon after the outbreak of war, had joined the Four Courts' division of the Veteran Corps, with whom he diligently marched and drilled. When one of his fellow-Veterans was shot and killed, however, he wasn't there. He'd been staying with Elizabeth in England – it was Easter week, 1916 – when the corps ran into trouble on its return from a route march. He caught the next boat back.

Half of Sackville Street had gone west by the time Henry rejoined his regiment in Dublin. Those with whom W. B. Yeats had been in the habit of exchanging polite meaningless words had succumbed to an endemic delirium of the brave – and the first sufferer was Dublin, which experienced the effects of all-out British shelling. It lost, among other buildings, its post office and Liberty Hall. Some people proceeded to lose their heads, among them an army-officer cousin of Elizabeth's named Captain Bowen-Colthurst. A well-known Dublin pacifist, Francis Sheehy-Skeffington, was taken up in the act of restraining would-be looters, in the wake of the Rising. On the night following his odd arrest he was obliged to accompany a military party through the streets of Dublin, and witnessed the shooting, by Captain Bowen-Colthurst, of a boy named Coade. Next morning, the

Captain organized the hasty execution, in the prison yard, of Sheehy-Skeffington and two of his fellow-prisoners (journalists unconnected with the nationalist movement). Bowen-Colthurst was later court-martialled and declared insane, but not before he'd been posted to Newry in command of troops.

The business greatly agitated his mother, Cousin Georgina, who hurried to Henry's Dublin flat in search of counsel which Henry wasn't really qualified to give, being merely an expert in Land Purchase. He put her in touch with the proper agency. Ireland, meanwhile, was in the process of acquiring sixteen martyrs, and Lady Gregory was advising ballad-makers to get their material up to date: 'Now let them rhyme out those that died,/With the three colours, yesterday.'

Elizabeth, nearing the end of her second year at Downe House, can't have been greatly affected by any of these events, though they may have underlined, for her, the ambiguity in the position of families like the Bowens (from Ireland but not exactly of it; not straightforwardly English either; and implicated, as far as each country was concerned, in the other's misdeeds). That summer, she stayed with Henry at Bowen's Court, with her Aunt Sarah Bowen, from Mitchelstown, keeping house for the pair of them. Henry was writing a book on Land Purchase, and had brought the manuscript to Co. Cork with him in a Gladstone bag. He was fifty-four. Two years later, when Elizabeth had been done with school for over a year, he married Mary Gwynn, daughter of a Clontarf doctor, and sister of some old friends of Henry's. Mary's brother Stephen Gwynn was an essayist and poet who had once been responsive to the stirring element in Ireland's past:

> I call to your mind Benburb,
> And the stubborn Ulster steel,
> Clonmel, and the glorious stand
> Of the younger Hugh O'Neill;
> And Owen dead at Derry
> And Cromwell loosed on the land . . .

He wrote that in 1903. 1916, which he saw in common with many others as a stab in England's gallant back, slightly changed his views. By 1919 he'd become an advocate of Dominion Home Rule – an objective described by Arthur Griffith as 'dead in its cradle', while the headier doctrine of republicanism flourished.

The marriage between Henry Bowen and Mary Gwynn seems to have been generally approved; under Mary's touch, Elizabeth noted, Henry's Merrion Street flat became 'very much less bleak'. Elizabeth continued to make her home with Aunt Laura at Harpenden, but spent part of each year at Bowen's Court, often accompanied by her cousin Audrey. The two were at an age when they thought nothing of driving forty miles over the mountains in an open cart in pursuit of diversion. Country-house and garrison dances and tennis parties abounded at the time, and drew all the eager young Anglo-Irish girls from miles around. The influx of young officers, detailed to suppress revolt, made for an increase in gaiety, at one level.

However – 'last night they trundled down the road,/The dead young soldier in his blood.' So Yeats observed. Sinn

Fein had only one object in view, (as de Valera put it), 'to make English rule absolutely impossible in Ireland'. And it was a popular movement, with a republican spirit prevailing everywhere. It was left to Elizabeth to record a counter-vailing spirit, that of 'big house' civility and *savoir-vivre*, in her novel of 1929, *The Last September*.

THREE

In *The Last September* (1929) Elizabeth Bowen is very pointed and illuminating on the efforts of upper-class ladies to turn a blind eye to bloodshed and disruption, to act as if they were in Kensington instead of Cork; and on the obtuseness of certain English incomers – army wives in particular, but also those bewildered by the complex relations existing between loyalist occupants of big houses and their rebel neighbours. She turns, as well, an astringent eye on the banal stratagems of girls in love with love. ('Common' behaviour is always one of her targets.) Has she appropriated any of her own feeling for Lois, the central character in the novel, and, the author tells us, not an autobiographical figure? We can find quite a few correspondences. Lois is one of those heroines who are far too edgy and complicated ever to be vulgarly infatuated. Her association with Gerald Lesworth, a young British officer attached to a nearby garrison, is rather tenuous and fraught with obstacles, on Lois's side at least. He – the constant, steadfast soldier figure – is surer about his feelings.

Elizabeth, at roughly the same age, found herself 'in love'

with a young lieutenant garrisoned in Ireland; an engagement of sorts followed, to which a stop was put after Aunt Edie (wife of Florence's brother George Colley) – then on holiday in Italy, where Elizabeth joined her – had had her say about the matter. It's the sort of drama all romantically-minded girls precipitate. In the book, it is Lady Naylor, of the house called Danielstown, who intervenes in the tiresome business between moneyless Lesworth and her niece Lois, before it gets out of hand. Lady Naylor is the type of managing relative whose function is to quash any improvident alliance proposed by a member of her family. In this case, it isn't especially difficult: she has only to enunciate the word 'nonsense', in a kind, social voice, for poor Gerald's head to be filled with doubts. *His* doubts, in conjunction with Lois's, finish the affair.

Lois, we're given to understand, became engaged for want of anything better to do; life at Danielstown, where a kind of aimlessness and malaise are in the air, doesn't meet her substantial requirements. Envisaging herself as Gerald's wife is one way to imagine a livelier future. Is there, perhaps, in the final confrontation between the would-be lovers, a shade too much fuss and whipped-up desperation? ' "Gerald, you'll kill me, just standing there ..." "I don't understand you," he cried in agony.' That sort of thing. If so, it's a very small flaw in a novel that positively hums with self-possession and perceptiveness.

The *bois dormant* is a recurring Bowen image (once actually attached to the 'big house' and its surrounding demesne), and it suits the romantic mood of *The Last September*. 'In those days,' we read on the opening page, 'girls wore crisp white skirts and transparent blouses clotted with white flowers; ribbons, threaded through with a view to appearance, appeared over their shoulders.' The novel is also concerned with disenchantment: there are things that everyone in the book has got to wake up to. You get people who go through life ineffectually; wrong commitments are entered into; being decent doesn't save you from disaster. Your fellow countrymen may turn on you.

What gives the Lois–Gerald relationship its special edge, of course, is the atmosphere of political tension in which it's located. Gerald, at any moment, may go to meet his death – as he does, in fact, after that keyed-up talk with Lois, with her aunt's discouraging comments ringing in his ears ('at her age, with her temperament, of course it is nice to love anyone . . . She cares for her drawing intensely'). By April 1919 Cork was one of the Irish counties under military control, and police and army barracks, and British patrols, were constant objects of attack. There's a real-life precedent for what happens to Gerald: in September 1919, at Fermoy (a town not far from Bowen's Court), a British soldier on patrol was shot and killed by Cork No. 2 Brigade of the Irish Volunteers. Violence upon the roads. (In reprisal, British Regulars overran and ransacked Fermoy: but that doesn't come into the Bowen story.)

Nineteen hundred and nineteen: the year Yeats singled out in his great meditation on destructiveness, loss and the creative instinct. 'Many ingenious lovely things are gone,' and more were to go, ancestral homes among them; a drunken soldiery was on the loose; and for the wagers of guerrilla warfare, a striking image is found: they 'are but weasels fighting in a hole'. Irish disorder has reached a pretty virulent pitch. *The Last September* is dated precisely to the following year, 1920. The British forces have gained a rowdy adjunct, dubbed the Black and Tans; at one point in the book, Lois, driving in a pony-and-trap, is obliged to turn hastily up a boreen to avoid a lorry full of these rogue irregulars. In what other ways do the troubles not quite impinge on her? A man in a trench coat, intent on Ireland's business, hurries by her one evening in her own demesne; a cache of guns may be buried in the lower plantation; an unnerving encounter with a gunman takes place in a derelict mill round the bend of a valley ('Inside the mill door, a high surge of nettles; one beam had rotted and come down, there was some debris of the roof').

Danielstown is Bowen's Court, unaltered; Lois, though, is a niece of the house, not child of it as Elizabeth was. (Did she have in mind, in creating Lois, that Georgian Miss Pretty who lived with her uncle and aunt at Bowen's Court, and made the hyacinth garden that lasted down to Elizabeth's day?) In her preface to the 1952 Knopf edition of *The Last September*, Elizabeth mentions her heroine's uninflamed attitude to Ireland's wrongs: wouldn't Lois – 'at her romantic age' – have felt the lure of revolutionary beliefs? The answer is that the war, for those who grew up in the 1914–18 period, satisfied any reasonable juvenile craving for upheaval: enough was enough. But the truth is probably that Elizabeth's temperament, and, by extension, Lois's, made her place her faith in inherited assets like houses and traditions of hospitality and a ceremonious approach to living. ('Not contributing to anarchy', as she said in a letter to Graham Greene, is an important part of the writer's function.) She thought that, however dubiously her ancestors and others had obtained their Irish holdings, they'd sufficiently enriched the life of the country to mitigate that initial injustice.

Hospitality: in *The Last September*'s final conflagration, 'the door stood hospitably open upon a furnace'. Many houses of the Anglo-Irish went up in flames as a destructive urge took hold of the republican movement. Elizabeth, in Italy in the spring of 1921, recuperating from her broken engagement, received from her father a letter instructing her to brace herself: three houses in the neighbourhood had already gone. Bowen's Court was spared, as it happened (in spite of its containing, among its collection, portraits of two of the villains of Irish history, Oliver Cromwell and William III), but its end was anticipated so intensely by Elizabeth that she must have written the ending of *The Last September* as a kind of exorcism.

In the book, there is some talk of sending Lois to a school of art, even though she's not particularly talented ('I think you're cleverer than you can draw, you know,' says a young woman visitor to Danielstown). To denote a way of marking time, the school of art isn't arbitrarily chosen. Elizabeth, who was better than average but probably not much, once spent two terms at the Central School of Arts and Crafts in Southampton Row in London. Art and poetry were two things she tried her hand at before relinquishing them in favour of prose. Did the first two smack too much of uncontrollable self-expression? 'I am dead against art's being self-expression,' she wrote in 1959. Any story worth its salt should 'detach itself from the author', something she was afraid her own didn't always do. But the best of them did.

By the time she was in her early twenties she had a clutch of stories, written in her Harpenden attic room, on a ninepenny block with lined pages; these went out to various magazines and promptly came back: a chastening experience not evaded by Elizabeth any more than anyone else. She wasn't unduly discouraged. In London, she lived at Queen's Gate with a great-aunt, Lady Allendale, and spent her evenings at places like the Poetry Bookshop, where she once attended a candlelit reading by Ezra Pound. The 1920s were getting under way.

It wasn't long before Elizabeth's career was taken in hand by Rose Macaulay, with whom she'd been put in touch by her old Downe House headmistress. A Bowen story was printed in the *Saturday Westminster*; Elizabeth found herself in a position to attend literary parties – and then Sidgwick and Jackson undertook to bring out a collection of her stories. *Encounters* appeared in 1923, and was favourably received. Justly? Well, Elizabeth's own eventual verdict on this and its successor, *Ann Lee's* – 'a blend of precosity and *naïveté*' – isn't likely to be disagreed with at present. When she came to reread her earliest stories (in 1949, for the preface to a new edition) she was struck by a certain frivolity and effervescence in them. She noted, rather critically, their attention to detail: the soft, furred edges of a tea-gown trapped in a wardrobe door; the parasols; the wisps of smoke from a small wood fire. Too pretty, she thought; but lively nevertheless, and illuminating at times. She was still learning; however, her stories showed at once a striking accomplishment in the matter of scenes and settings. It was just that character, in its solid and enduring aspect, interested her, as yet, rather less than the characteristic pose.

These stories are exercises in observation, rounded out by guesswork: sketches, if you like, in which an ironic repudiation of absurd behaviour is paramount. Mockery, 'the small smile of one who, herself, knows better', is never very far away. The author is hardest on people who go in for archness and effusiveness, or exhibit a fearful sensitivity. Her own soundness of outlook – a quality that made a good base for the experiments in intricacy she carried out later – is strongly in evidence.

Her first novel, *The Hotel* (1928) is perhaps less successful; it is a rather mannered and episodic piece of work, and it owes a bit too much to Virginia Woolf (whose first allusion to Elizabeth, in her diary, has to do with the fact that Lady Ottoline Morrell is reading a book 'by Eth Bowen who tries to write like me'). She, along with Henry James and one or two others, was an influence Elizabeth had to absorb before arriving at a style unmistakably her own.

The setting of this novel – a hotel on the Italian Riviera – enabled Elizabeth to poke fun at the social life of such places, full of potty English residents: the ecstasies of misunderstanding, the burning attachments. Its central figure is a girl, like Lois Farquhar of *The Last September*, in a semi-somnambulant state. (Intelligence temporarily displaced by some kind of torpor seems to be associated by Elizabeth Bowen with late adolescence in interesting girls: the *bois dormant* motif.) Sydney Warren makes a wrong decision about her future, becoming inappropriately engaged, but she comes to her senses in time. The setting, we may note, is the one in which Elizabeth's own first engagement fell apart. In her fiction, she rarely uses any part of her life without transforming it; but many oblique connections *are* to be found. Indeed, they can't be avoided. Fiction, Elizabeth said, 'is bound to be transposed autobiography', though 'it may be this at so many removes as to defeat ordinary recognition'.

Her first engagement had fallen apart, but she didn't waste too much time before embarking on another. Through her Aunt Gertrude (Audrey Fiennes's mother) who lived at Bloxham, in Oxfordshire, Elizabeth had met a young ex-Army captain named Alan Cameron: a First World War veteran suffering from the effects of gas poisoning. He'd been educated at Radley and Oxford, and in 1921 he was made Assistant Secretary for Education for Northamptonshire. He and Elizabeth got on terrifically. They strode about the countryside discussing literature. The next thing was, they got engaged – and this engagement prospered. They were married at Blisworth, Northamptonshire, in August 1923 – Elizabeth in a home-made dress of amber crêpe de Chine – and moved into a horrid little house not far from Northampton (as a Colley aunt described it). Here *Ann Lee's* and *The Hotel* were written.

Elizabeth continued to visit Bowen's Court whenever she could; some days, she says, she caught a train to London; in the spring and late summer she would travel to Italy or France. Otherwise, she wrote: at a knee-hole table in a projecting window, with a view of garden allotments stretching in front of her. What marriage gave her, above all, was a permanent position, a sense of living somewhere; before that, since Herbert Place, it had been a matter of being shunted here and there, at the whim of adults: from Downe to Harpenden, from Cork to Italy, from London to Bloxham. Elizabeth's farouche quality – a quality she ascribes not only to herself, but to only children, to the Anglo-Irish isolated in their big houses, and to an extent to writers – began to diminish, on the surface at any rate. She remained farouche at heart, perhaps, but gained from her married state, as well as from her exhilarating authorship, a new confidence and aplomb. Under the influence of her husband she took to wearing better clothes, or at least clothes more in keeping with her strong-boned Anglo-Irish appearance, tailored suits and dresses and well-made shoes. She would have looked simply silly in anything picturesque.

Victoria Glendinning, in her biography of Elizabeth Bowen, lists the people who fully appreciated Alan Cameron: they included Elizabeth's father and her cousins Audrey Fiennes and Noreen Colley. It's necessary to single out his champions, to counteract the rather disparaging view of him that grew up in certain circles. He remains, though, a difficult person to pin down, largely because of the contradictory opinions held by those who knew him. He was hearty and sensitive, a conscientious host and a solitary diner, a constant prop for his wife and a trial to her literary friends. He lowered the spirits of dinner guests with his intolerable anecdotes, or raised them by means of his charm and intelligence. He was forceful and ineffectual. He was witty and dull, a kind-hearted person, a bore, a philistine and a fat old blimp. He inspired loyalty and aversion. Elizabeth's affection for him was a mystery to some, and perfectly understandable to others. What are we to make of all this? One thing seems certain – that, having started out as, in a sense, the dominant partner in the marriage, Alan Cameron came to feel slightly out of his depth in the literary milieu relished by Elizabeth, and retreated more and more into a pose of plainness and self-mockery (dubbing himself 'Alfred the Good', for example). We remember Thomas Quayne, in *The Death of the Heart*, lurking in his study until his wife Anna's exasperating callers have taken themselves off.

After two years in the Midlands, the Camerons moved to Old Headington, Oxfordshire, on Alan's appointment as Secretary for Education for the city of Oxford. In place of their horrid little house they acquired a charming one, a converted coach-house blue-washed inside, and with an iron staircase. To this house (called Waldencote) came new friends like the Buchans, Lord David Cecil and Maurice Bowra. Elizabeth was in her element in Oxford; the atmosphere – learning tempered with sociability – kept her on her mettle. *Ann Lee's* came out in 1927, and a novel, *The Hotel*, a year later (published by Constable). A third volume of stories, *Joining Charles*, followed in 1929; and also in that year appeared *The Last September*.

Elizabeth, who'd doubted whether she possessed the right sort of mind to tackle a novel, found that she did. She'd suspected herself of flightiness in her approach to fiction: 'I could spotlight, but not illumine steadily.' She is still spotlighting a bit in *The Hotel*, but by the time of *The Last Sep-*

tember her faculty for steady illumination has become apparent. This novel, it's true, with its romantic, elegiac feeling and its sharp social interludes, reaches a level of accomplishment not easily regained ('Of all my books', she said, this one 'is nearest my heart'). It gets its force, in part, from the strong Irish theme and all its unstated complications, and also from the feeling invested in the re-creation of girlhood summers (all of them compressed into that one summer of 1920) – and, by comparison, its successor of 1931, *Friends and Relations*, can't but seem a little watered-down.

Friends and Relations opens with a well-conducted Cheltenham wedding: lilies, kid gloves, marquee and all. Laurel Studdart, the sunnier of two sisters, is marrying Edward Tilney, whose mother, Lady Elfrida, hasn't an unimpeachable past. She once misbehaved with a big-game hunter. Janet Studdart, more of a dark horse than her sister, proceeds, after Laurel's wedding, to marry the one-time game-hunter's nephew, Rodney Meggatt. A web of family connections is thereby set up. At its centre is the unacknowledged, or very belatedly acknowledged, sexual attraction between Janet and Edward, which comes to nothing. The prospect of sexual fulfilment is relinquished by this pair in a mood of intensity – and somewhat evasively, it must be added. There's still a tinge of unnecessary delicacy about the author's handling of this matter.

The creation of social comedy, on the other hand, came naturally to her; and *Friends and Relations* is memorable for its portrait of an awful, irrepressible female adolescent called Theodora Thirdman. Theodora, large, bespectacled and full of misplaced aplomb, is destined to grow into an overbearing lesbian lady. A different kind of awfulness afflicts poor Pauline, the orphan niece in *To the North* (1932): with her urbane uncle, who isn't captivated, she is 'diligently little-girlish; whimsicality distorted their conversation'. From such comic imperfections the adolescent Portia in *The Death of the Heart* is free: to her is allocated another, and more important, role in the novel, as we shall see. But usually, in Elizabeth's view of this age-group, there's a strong element of Downe House dryness.

To the North (published by Gollancz) contains another characteristically risible Bowen figure: the overweening aunt who likes to have a finger in every pie. The name of this particular interferer is Lady Waters. For all its inter-mittent comic vigour, however, this is a more disquieting novel than its predecessor. The north wind blows chill. The book is centred on two young women, sisters-in-law, one a widow, who share a house in St John's Wood, 'that airy uphill neighbourhood where the white and buff-coloured houses, pilastered or gothic, seem to have been built in a grove'. The elder, more lightweight and worldly of the two is Cecilia Summers; it's she who, unknowingly, disrupts her young sister-in-law's life by introducing into it a barrister she's met casually on a train. Emmeline Summers, as has often been noted, belongs among Elizabeth Bowen's alarming innocents, people whose unworldliness is po-tentially lethal. Markie, the man – this name, which he has engraved on his cigarette case, immediately establishes him as someone un-serious and a little flashy – exemplifies an-other Bowen type: wayward and undependable. He, like all of his kind, is engagingly but fatally deficient in moral fibre. To this character 'the dynamic Maurice Bowra', one of Elizabeth's close Oxford friends, contributed his looks.

'The kid and the cad': this merry expression of Seán O'Faoláin's does as well as any to describe the fated alliance set up by Elizabeth in her fiction on more than one occasion. (O'Faoláin's admiration for Elizabeth has always been tempered with affectionate mockery: a style of writing she resorts to a great deal, for example, he irreverently calls 'the Bowen 707 or Take-Off style.') When kids and cads get entangled with one another, it's to the detriment of both. Emmeline, though she's not as young as all that (nothing like as young as Portia Quayne, for instance), has retained a childlike capacity for wholeheartedness which does her no good at all. ('It is not only our fate, but our business, to lose innocence,' Elizabeth wrote briskly on one occasion; in *To the North* she seems to be saying: look what happens to those who don't properly make it their business.)

Emmeline, as H. G. Wells remarked in a letter to Elizabeth, is charming. (She's short-sighted, as Elizabeth was, and also prefers to see life through a haze rather than wear her glasses.) So is Markie, in his devious way, not least because his actions are dictated by a sensuous approach to living. What gets between them is simply a disparity of temperaments – one uncalculating and the other incalculable. As always in Elizabeth Bowen, it's a dire conjunction. Their relation with one another is tending all along towards some exorbitant finale, which duly occurs. 'An immense idea of departure' takes hold of Emmeline: this is one way of putting it. It couldn't, indeed, be more immense; she is about to crash the car she is driving. 'Poor Emmeline!' Elizabeth said towards the end of her life. 'It was inevitable.'

This overwhelming action of Emmeline's is accommodated, without strain or fuss, within a framework of conventional social goings-on presented coolly and divertingly ('There was a sort of girl there, like a bad illustration to Hans Andersen'). A Jamesian intricacy of feeling, and a kind of *bois dormant* romanticism, complicate the quizzical, disabused, 1920s manner which is exemplified in early Bowen fiction as much as anywhere.

Elizabeth's father Henry Bowen retired from the Bar in 1928; two years later, after a short physical illness which brought with it a relapse into the old disturbed mental state, he died. He died at Bowen's Court in May 1930; Elizabeth, who'd been summoned some weeks earlier, would sit with him in the evenings, after coming in from a walk in the demesne with the poet Stephen Gwynn – one of the people gathered in the house, 'to say goodbye to Henry'. 'When he was dead,' Elizabeth went on (her account of her father's death comes towards the end of *Bowen's Court*), 'I went upstairs to the Long Room, where I walked up and down . . . Like all the Bowens whose dates are known, I had inherited before I was thirty-one.'

'Oh, you, when are you going back to your ancient Irish castle?' Virginia Woolf would say teasingly to Elizabeth, when the two women had become friends; and, indeed, Elizabeth went to stay at Bowen's Court whenever she could, sometimes alone, sometimes with Alan, often in the company of friends. She became celebrated for her hospitality, both in Ireland and England (Stephen Spender, for instance, remembers her most keenly as a hostess). Innumerable visitors to Bowen's Court recalled the pleasures, and sometimes the discomforts, of staying in an Irish big house. It was apt to be cold in winter, when condensation affected the windows and damp got into the beds. There was no bathroom. The lavatories – *c.* 1860 – were rather primitive. Never mind, such things were negligible in comparison with the talent for sociability inherited by Elizabeth and here exercised by her to the full. (Keeping the estate accounts and other practical matters fell to the lot of Alan, who tackled them willingly and efficiently.)

In summer, visitors assembled on the wide front steps to soak up the sun, walked or drove in the nearby countryside, played tennis or bathed: in the River Blackwater, or, further afield, at seaside Youghal. The evenings were given over to card or paper-games, always an enthusiasm of Elizabeth's. (She mischievously invented a game called Bad Parties, which involved plotting out the most frightful combination of guests – 'though they may be nice individually' – you could bring together. By this means an atmosphere of hilarity must have been produced.) Bowen's Court, however, much as they loved it, was something of a financial burden to the Camerons; Elizabeth has written feelingly about the efforts of 'big house' people to keep the roof intact. She is also amusing, in her essay on 'The Moores', about the landowner pursued all over the place by what she calls 'fateful letters in dogged handwriting, sure to begin inside, "Sir, I am sorry to tell you …" ' – letters bearing an Irish stamp.

FOUR

Elizabeth Bowen came in on the tail-end of Bloomsbury, of which she'd been conscious throughout the twenties, but she was never interested in allying herself exclusively with any group, either social or literary. 'What an agreeable life we all had, seeing each other *without* being "a group",' she remarked in a letter to William Plomer, congratulating him on the publication of *At Home* in 1958. In that book, he mentions the funeral of King George V, in January 1937, recalling how, in the afternoon, he 'went on to the Woolves, where I found Elizabeth Bowen and Iris Origo and Ethel Smyth . . .' Elizabeth couldn't remember going to tea at Virginia's on that occasion, though the rest of the day remained clearly with her:

. . . My cousin Noreen [Noreen Colley], who was staying with us, and Billy Buchan [son of Lord and Lady Tweedsmuir, then lodging with the Camerons] and I had got up at 4 a.m. to watch the procession in the Edgware Road, and I remember nothing else about the afternoon except being anaesthetized by tiredness, plus in vain looking for food for that night's dinner (to which I do remember you and Tom Eliot came) with all shops shut: a condition I'd forgotten to foresee.

She finally wheedled a large veal-and-ham pie (at a black

market price) out of the chef at a 'little restaurant in the understructure of Baker Street Station where I sometimes ate', and the dinner party was, as ever, a success.

It had taken some time for this loose network of vivid friendships, in which Elizabeth played her part, to build up. Elizabeth, for example, had got to know Lady Ottoline Morrell in the early 1930s, and it was at a tea-party in her Gower Street house that Elizabeth first met Virginia Woolf. The famous novelist, got up in lavender muslin and a floppy hat, confided to Elizabeth her intention of making some gooseberry-flavoured ice-cream. Later, when she'd had Elizabeth to tea, she tersely jotted down her attributes: a stammer, shyness and conventionality.

She's still calling Elizabeth 'conventional' in June 1933, but things gradually looked up between them; in November of that year we find another note, 'Eth Bowen, improving'. She visited Oxford, and was taken for a drive in the Cotswolds by Elizabeth and Susan Buchan (Lady Tweedsmuir). The following spring, when she and Leonard Woolf were travelling in Ireland, they spent a night at Bowen's Court, 'where, to our horror,' she wrote to her sister Vanessa Bell, 'we found the Connollys – a less appetizing pair I have never seen out of the zoo . . .' As for Bowen's Court – 'a great barrack of grey stone', she found it, 'yet with character and charm'. (She wasn't greatly taken with Vita Sackville-West's Knole either: 'too little conscious beauty for my taste'.) The cracks in the grand pianos, the stains on the walls, and what she unfairly called 'the faked old portraits' didn't escape her relentless eye. Neither did the furniture come up to scratch: 'clumsy, solid, cut out of single wood'.

It's the usual story of Anglo-Irish dilapidation (however, photographs show a more imposing house, in rather better repair, than we'd expect after the Woolf depiction). Still, a good turkey supper was put in front of her, and Alan – 'a good humoured, bolt-eyed, fat, hospitable man' – was evidently at his most affable.

Cyril Connolly's view of the occasion is rather more circumspect. ('Elizabeth's house' – where he and his American wife Jean were staying – 'lovely but rather forlorn', he noted in his journal for that year.) Mentioning the arrival of the Woolfs, he praises Virginia's appearance, adds that she and her husband 'seemed shocked by Jean's dress' and records their preoccupation with plans and motoring. Nearly everyone who knew her alludes to Virginia Woolf's habit of subjecting people to interrogation once she'd got hold of a topic that interested her (her 'consuming curiosity' about the details of people's lives); at Bowen's Court, according to Cyril Connolly, she kept demanding that Elizabeth should explain unnatural vice to her: 'I mean what do they *do?*' (Elizabeth's answer isn't supplied.) The subject can hardly have been a mystery or a novelty to her, at fifty-two, and after her close association with Lytton Strachey and others. Elizabeth, who probably wasn't at all discomposed by this *enfant terrible* behaviour, always urged Virginia Woolf to revisit Bowen's Court, but she never did. Nor, it seems, did she manage another trip to Old Headington; Elizabeth, in a letter, describes herself and Maurice Bowra having tea together, and says they spent a lot of time wishing that Virginia would come to Oxford, driving suddenly down as she had half-promised she might.

In the same letter, Elizabeth mentions having been to Rome in the early autumn (the year is 1934), and sitting in a grandstand to watch Mussolini on a white horse reviewing police, dogs, bands, tanks: 'that was awful'. Considerably more amusing was a waiter, who, when Elizabeth didn't understand an item in the **menu**, 'flapped his elbows like wings, made cooing noises then split himself down the breastbone with his thumbnail to show it was half a pigeon'. (She had an audience with the pope, but doesn't elaborate on that.)

Maurice Bowra, whom everyone remembers as forceful and flamboyant, seems to have written in a style at odds with his personality: bland and non-committal. This, at any rate, is the manner in which he records his impressions of Elizabeth in her Oxford days: she was handsome, he says (in his book called *Memories 1898–1939*), 'in an unusual way, with a face that indicated both mind and character . . . She had the fine style of a great lady, who on rare occasions was not shy of slapping down impertinence . . . With all her sensibility and imagination, she had a masculine intelligence which was fully at home in large subjects and general ideas.' It's a pretty colourless portrait of a friend – still, interesting to see that a 'Grand Duchess' manner wasn't unavailable to the person Virginia Woolf dubbed 'silent and stuttering'.

How did Alan Cameron strike Maurice Bowra? He's still not giving much away: 'an attentive host who had much interest in academic and intellectual matters', is the summing-up Elizabeth's husband gets. The two of them, he tells us, 'added a very distinctive note to our lives'. This seems true enough. For one thing, there were sojourns at Bowen's Court, all very interesting and animated. Both Bowra and Cyril Connolly, visiting there on separate occasions, were taken by Elizabeth to view the ruins of Mitchelstown Castle (scene of the garden party she attended in August 1914) – a casualty of the Civil War, first commandeered and then fired by republican forces in the summer of 1922. The same detachment then moved westward to occupy Bowen's Court for a short time, but left it intact; enabling it to function, throughout the thirties, as a kind of outpost to the literary worlds of London and Oxford.

To Elizabeth's Irish house they all made their way: Lord David Cecil ('my oldest, securest friend'), William Plomer, Roger Senhouse, Isaiah Berlin, Stuart Hampshire, Raymond Mortimer, Henry Reed, Rosamond Lehmann, Seán O'Faoláin, Goronwy Rees, Humphry House ... With the last, whom she first met at lunch in Oxford with Maurice Bowra, Elizabeth had fallen immoderately in love (as immoderately as Emmeline does in *To the North*). The year of this emotional onslaught was 1933; the time was right for Elizabeth to experience some productive disturbance in her well-ordered life. Whatever the nature of the bond between her and Alan (Victoria Glendinning says), 'it was not primarily a physical one'. It has, indeed, been suggested that Elizabeth remained *virgo intacta* up until this year, her thirty-fourth. Whatever the truth of the matter, it seems certain that nothing so crass as a 'sexual awakening' overtook her, though she undoubtedly gave way to sexual pressures. More than half of her novelist's mind would have been considering, objectively, not only the ups and downs, but the *quality* of the whole intoxicating affair.

There were difficulties and complications in plenty for the novelist to savour. Humphry House, who'd been a Fellow and Lecturer in English Literature at Wadham College, Oxford, since 1931, was Elizabeth's junior by eight or nine years. He was also engaged to be married. The marriage duly took place at the end of 1933, but his entanglement with Elizabeth wasn't immediately affected by it. Elizabeth knew his wife Madeleine and, at some level, got on with her (perhaps not all that well, however: on one occasion Madeleine House took umbrage when Elizabeth sent her a tea service as a present, believing this to be a veiled allusion to her fitness for domesticity, and nothing else). On Elizabeth's side of the business, Alan had to be kept in the dark – at least to the extent where his peace of mind would not suffer; we have no information as to where exactly this point came. In this affair, no one's marriage was to be endangered: that was the first rule. However, it didn't take long for Elizabeth and Humphry House to get at cross purposes with one another, and for much unease and exasperation to be engendered (perhaps her intemperance of feeling was too much for him, as Emmeline's was for Markie, in the novel that had come out the previous year).

When he stayed at Bowen's Court in 1935 Humphry House was summoned home early by a series of telegrams from his pregnant wife announcing that the roof had blown off the house; Elizabeth complained in a letter to William Plomer – in words for once not very well chosen – that the whole thing was 'a bit of a barren muddle'. William Plomer himself had left only a short time earlier. 'You were very positively missed,' Elizabeth told him. She found herself in rather low spirits; her cousin Noreen had just gone too. She and Jim Gates (a Bowen's Court neighbour and friend of Elizabeth's) had driven Noreen to Limerick Junction, on the other side of the Galtees:

... when we got back here we felt very depressed, so we had some whiskey and put on the wireless, right in the middle of a lady called Helen Simpson broadcasting a review of *The House in Paris*, a coincidence which seemed very fatal and funny and pleased Jim very much.

The House in Paris (1935) was Elizabeth's fifth novel, and it's centred on a gigantic piece of bad behaviour: getting pregnant by your friend's fiancé rather than your own. This novel, perhaps, aims to subvert the idea of love as a rational passion, which Elizabeth (in her book on *English Novelists*, and with reference to Fielding) found flourishing in the eighteenth century in particular, but also saw as a principle governing, and in a sense limiting, the English novel in general. Only the French and the Russians, she claimed, were properly alive to its inherent disorder and pain.

The long middle section of *The House in Paris*, called 'The Past', goes back ten years to recount the experiences of Karen Michaelis, daughter of a conventional London family, once a student-boarder at Mme Fisher's exclusive guest-house in Paris, and subsequently impelled towards an illicit association with the unlikely fiancé of Mme Fisher's daughter Naomi. Unlikely? Well, yes; everything in the book is geared to show up that alliance for what it is: a chimera.

Nothing more urgent than a kind of hankering after safety has caused Max Ebhart, a young, half-Jewish banker and friend of Mme Fisher's, to propose to Naomi Fisher who, lacking allure, has made herself dependable. Later, in the course of his affair with Karen, Max is moved to compare poor Naomi to a pillow, an item of domestic comfort he has decided he can do without.

Karen, who is engaged to someone else, is in every way a better bet than her friend Naomi – cleverer, prettier, richer – as Naomi's mother doesn't hesitate to point out to Max, filling him with such doubts and apprehensions that he goes off to sever an artery in his wrist. Before this, there's been a Co. Cork interlude, when Karen visits an Irish aunt and uncle (Uncle Bill, a casualty of Ireland's disorder, keeps on the wall of his present house some photographs of the old one, burnt). Here, the narrative partakes of the countryside's 'disturbing repose'; Karen, like other Bowen girls, is in a half-entranced state not unconnected with deferred erotic feeling. (Why does Elizabeth, in *The Last September*, have a character say that sex seems irrelevant in Ireland? This isn't at all the same thing as the point she makes in her preface to *Uncle Silas*, when she puts her finger on a persistent facet of Irish fiction: its sexlessness. Of the Le Fanu story she says: 'No force from any one of the main characters runs into the channel of sexual feeling' – and in this it's typical.)

It's the *bois dormant* again: in the chapter on Places, in *Pictures and Conversations* (1974), Elizabeth draws our attention to this sinister-fairytale quality of *The House in Paris*, but ascribes it specifically to the claustrophobic room of an invalid, Mme Fisher – bedridden in the parts of the novel entitled 'The Present'. As a meddler, this character, malignant and intriguing, is on a different plane from the earlier opinionated aunts. There is rather more of the witch about her. She is continually ironic at her daughter's expense. 'The Present' is cast in a mode of sedate social comedy. The paths of two children, one of them Karen's (long since adopted) cross briefly at this house in Paris, which holds such significance for one, and none at all for the other. Henrietta, the uninvolved child, is merely on her way to join her grandmother in the South of France; she has stumbled, unawares, into an oblique drama. The other, Leopold, is waiting for his mother, Karen, who fails to turn up. Her husband turns up instead.

The affair between Karen and Max, which is of short duration, is enacted at Boulogne and Hythe, which warrant a trip apiece. The conception of Leopold is achieved at Hythe. The character of Max Ebhart, who is rather bleak and foreign, was prompted (we are to gather) by a person whom Elizabeth didn't know at all well; we needn't assume there is anything of Humphry House in him, any more than Karen resembles *her* (however tempting it is to see a parallel between the nerve-racked threesome of the novel, and the events surrounding Elizabeth while she wrote it). However, Victoria Glendinning suggests that Naomi Fisher, about whom there's more than a touch of the doormat, may owe something to Humphry House's wife, or at least to Elizabeth's obstinate conception of her. Elizabeth was apt to attribute all her lover's troubles and agitations of mind to what she called over-domesticity – at one point she describes his 'queer little claustrophobic house, full of the little anxious blonde wife, and little plain blonde babies', as 'something between a dolls' house and a rabbit hutch'. It's funny, but not quite kind.

Some months after his flurried exit from Bowen's Court, Humphry House left England for a time with his family. 'I think the prospect of going to India is upsetting him,' Elizabeth wrote to William Plomer after she'd announced that she and Humphry had 'had an awful row which is so sad: I am not a quarreller but really I don't think it was my fault.' She hated 'his going off to India under a blight'. However, they must have patched things up pretty quickly, for she's able to report to William Plomer, a few months later, that, 'Humphry is having an awful time in Calcutta: he is in hospital with flu and dysentery combined: his inside's been awful for two months ... The whole job and life sound pretty futile and futureless . . . I rather hope he'll come home. Though to *what* I don't quite know.' In the event, he stuck it out for two years or so; when he came back, he and Elizabeth stayed on excellent terms, though the affair had long since run its course. She and he went to Brighton for a day (early in August 1939), and visited a pier entertainment called '1001 laughs for 2d', where Elizabeth submitted to 'being biffed on the head by a sudden skeleton arm'. 'I don't react at all well to that sort of thing and it gave me palpitations.' Humphry House's well-being continued to be a matter of concern to her.

Elizabeth seems to have had a busy time in 1935. We find her, for example, reviewing fiction for the *New Statesman*, turn about with Peter Quennell, and complaining that, 'It is a perfectly awful business.' Virginia Woolf invited her to Rodmell at some point during that summer, and there's a letter in which she expresses her disappointment at not being able to go ('I did fearfully want to.') A sense of duty kept her in Oxford, where a conference of foreign educationalists was taking place under Alan's direction: 'I am so seldom a useful wife to Alan, and it did begin to appear that it really would be rather mean of me to go away leaving him overrun with people he had to be genial to.'

The foreign educationalists were entertained by being taken for a drive across the Cotswolds in a file of taxis. Elizabeth found the conference 'very queer: I wonder if they are all like that?' When it was over, she and Alan visited Wales, which didn't appeal greatly to her, in spite of her remote Welsh ancestry. 'Mountains depend so much on where they are put and in Wales they seem to be in one's mouth the whole time and have a scrubby, gritty surface.' A trip to Dieppe was squeezed into that summer too; it included a gala and a lot of drinking of calvados. 'Places are so exciting,' Elizabeth wrote to Virginia Woolf; 'the only proper experiences one has. I believe I may only write novels for the pleasure of saying where people are.'

We find her making a similar assertion nearly forty years later, in *Pictures and Conversations*: 'Am I not,' she asks, 'manifestly a writer for whom places loom large?' What has prompted the question is the failure, as she sees it, of reviewers and commentators on Elizabeth Bowen to pay proper attention to this important aspect of her literary impulse. Topography, for her, is 'what gives fiction its verisimilitude'. 'Nothing can happen nowhere.' Bowen terrain

– her term – shifts about between Co. Cork and London, Oxford and Kent, with occasional sallies abroad. All these locales are transfigured by her heady, acute and compelling perception of them.

As far as her stories are concerned, her electrifying use of atmosphere begins to be apparent in the 1941 volume, *Look at All Those Roses*, before receiving its fullest expression in the famous wartime stories collected under the title of *The Demon Lover* (1945). The stories' concern with the effects of places on characters, and the relegating of characters to the places they deserve are well noted by Hermione Lee in her valuable study of Elizabeth Bowen's work (published in 1981). Places, indeed, may have a moral implication imposed on them – hence all the new dispiriting houses in the stories, the flawed or vulnerable old family homes, the gimcrack, the bogus and the adulterated. Elizabeth Bowen, after her 1920s frivolity and smartness, quickly latched on to the troubling, *déraciné* spirit of the next decade, and embodied it most distinctively in the story called 'The Disinherited', from *The Cat Jumps* (1934). There's an air of late-night, provincial jadedness about this story, in which a corrupt poor relation 'sells her kisses' to her aunt's bleak chauffeur.

1935 was also the year the Camerons moved to London. Alan had been appointed Secretary to the Central Council of School Broadcasting at the BBC. In July (before the educational conference), Elizabeth mentioned to Virginia Woolf that she'd been househunting in London,

and also having people come to view ours. The agent rings up and strange hostile people with money to lay out are let in and come poking and pottering around. It feels odd – with strange mutters, from upstairs and everywhere, from people who have come to look for cracks in the walls.

She had, in fact, already found the house they would move into: No. 2, Clarence Terrace, Regent's Park, a corner house (early nineteenth-century), from the windows of which you could see 'the park lake with those coloured-sailed boats and a great many trees'. There was also a plan (which came into effect) to have the Tweedsmuirs' son William Buchan as a lodger (they were going to Canada and he, aged nineteen, was to study film-making at Elstree under Alfred Hitchcock). Although Elizabeth had never liked the idea of having a lodger in the house, she thought it might work in this case, 'as we are all very independent and sociable and not likely to want to sit on top of one another'. Also, it would help with the rent.

The move from Waldencote was duly effected late in 1935, and William Buchan installed. 2, Clarence Terrace is the house everyone associates with Elizabeth Bowen; not least because she put it into her novel of 1938, *The Death of the Heart*. (This was the book that nearly made her a popular, as well as an acclaimed, author. As Ivy Compton-Burnett remarked sardonically, 'People keep writing to her about the death of their hearts.') She changed nothing but 'Clarence', which becomes 'Windsor', and observed that (in its summer setting), 'the house offered that ideal mould for living into which life so seldom pours itself.' Streams of clever friends and admirers came to visit Elizabeth at Clarence Terrace. Alan, arriving home from the BBC, and being confronted with rows of Homburgs hanging on pegs, gave his wife's callers the collective title of 'Black Hats'. Here, as at Bowen's Court, Elizabeth shone as a hostess, even if, at times, it looked as though the naughty paper-game, Bad Parties, had influenced a guest list or two of her own. If she did invite, together, those who didn't exactly hit it off, it was simply because, as a novelist, she was interested in people's behaviour. Mischief-making didn't come into it.

Christmas, as usual, was spent at Bowen's Court that year, Alan returning to London on 28 December, leaving Elizabeth (and Noreen Colley) to attend a meet which had been arranged as a special treat for them. Elizabeth has left a description of the hunt ball that year at Bowen's Court:

... perfect. It was what I used to imagine when I was ten that a party here ought to be like. It was extremely gorgeous and uninane, as the band and trampling made talk impossible. Electric light was rigged up for the night, so that the house was ablaze inside, which I had never seen before. It was not at all a smart ball but very gay and in its own way what you would call stylish. We danced in the drawing-room for which red velvet curtains were borrowed for the occasion. ...

William Plomer, to whom these impressions were confided, had lately contributed to the *New Statesman* a poem called 'The Murder on the Downs' which Elizabeth and her cousin Noreen read that Christmas at Bowen's Court, with considerable relish ('It really is very *very* good'). Plomer himself has described 'The Murder on the Downs' as a poem 'about an erotic murder committed in daylight, in fine weather, on the Sussex Downs'. It's a quasi-ballad, rather heartless and jaunty, in an effective way, about the dreadful act (an imaginary one) which provides its subject:

> Under a sky without a cloud
> Lay the still unruffled sea,
> And in the bracken like a bed
> The murderee.

The point of the poem is that the victim has more than half acquiesced in her own destruction. When he came to look at it more than twenty years later – as he recounts in *At Home* – it struck William Plomer that the mood in which his murderer and victim performed their parts was simply a reflection of the prevailing mood of the period, 'compulsive violence ... unreasoning surrender'. Or was that to read too much into it? He didn't really think so. As well as 'The Murder on the Downs' (a title smacking of the contemporary vogue for detective fiction: it is very close to *The Menace on the Downs* by Miles Burton, who also, coincidentally, wrote a novel called *The Cat Jumps*), Plomer wrote a number of ballads and poems in which the sinister and the grotesque are playfully treated. Looking back at these, he saw them as symptomatic: 'by-products of an uneasy time'.

Elizabeth, who admired 'The Murder on the Downs', as we've seen, displayed a similar tendency, especially pronounced during the thirties, to incorporate into her short fiction episodes straight out of the popular press. The chauffeur, Prothero, in 'The Disinherited', for example, is lumbered with a melodramatic history (he's an undetected murderer); and elsewhere we find lurid accidents and murders zestfully re-created as ghost stories, comic-horror

pieces ('One of Mrs Bentley's hands was found in the library
. . . But the fingers were in the drawing-room') or psycho-
logical dramas ('Himself they had all – always – de-
precated').

Elizabeth Bowen's attraction to the supernatural, which,
austerely, she kept out of her novels, finds an outlet in
stories like these, in which it often acts as an invigorating
force. When the idea is not to explore to the fullest the
power of suggestion (as in 'The Cat Jumps'), or to devise an
embodiment for the numinous, she has fun with her ghosts.
In 'The Cheery Soul', for example, a playful spirit – in life a
drunken cook – leaves cryptic messages about fish-kettles,
and rude injunctions to her ex-employers.

'Uneasy', is William Plomer's word for the period between
the wars; Elizabeth uses it too, in *To the North*, when she
calls Emmeline a 'stepchild of her uneasy century'. She
wasn't, however, preoccupied with contemporary history
or the unease it generated, to the extent of allying herself
with any movement to better things, and certainly didn't
feel herself 'hounded by external events', in the way that
Stephen Spender (for example) did. (He uses this phrase in
his autobiography *World Within World*.) Something in her
temperament precluded her from taking a socialist view,
and she found the godlessness of her slightly younger contemporaries rather dispiriting. (Bloomsbury, too, struck her
in this way; at least in retrospect.) To call her Conservative
or Church of Ireland, though, creates a wrong impression –
it was more that these institutions were roughly in line with
her feeling for order and tradition.

FIVE

At the start of 1936 Elizabeth sent a bunch of pink and yellow tulips to Virginia Woolf, who was in bed with flu; that friendship by now was well established, though it never became exactly intimate – not surprisingly, considering the seventeen years' difference in age between the two, and the eminence of the elder. Other friendships of Elizabeth's flourished or foundered in season. Virginia Woolf, in her diary, records bumping into Rose Macaulay in the street, and finding her agitated by Elizabeth's apparent disinclination to see her: she'd called at Clarence Terrace to collect something, when Elizabeth was supposed to be out, and found a party in progress.

The diarist attributes Rose Macaulay's distress largely to her own state of mind. Certainly it seems unlikely that Elizabeth, who never underrated the help she had received from Rose Macaulay at the start of her career, would have wished to act slightingly towards the other author. Reviewing Rose Macaulay's book on E. M. Forster in the *New Statesman* in 1936, she commended it in the warmest possible terms: 'outstanding . . . excellent . . . brilliantly done'.

These are hardly the words of someone who's taken against the author of the book in question.

Still, her biographer, Victoria Glendinning, has remarked that it wasn't unknown for close women friends of Elizabeth's to find themselves suddenly discarded. Sometimes the reason was plain, as in the case of Nancy Spain, who apparently made some kind of pass at Elizabeth, and whom, moreover, Alan detested – but more often it wasn't. Perhaps her behaviour in this respect was simply due to a trait carried over from childhood: as she says in her essay 'Out of a Book', 'children abandon people . . . with a simplicity that really ought not to be hurting . . .' Virginia Woolf herself at one point thought she'd been abandoned by Elizabeth (wrongly, as it turned out); her diary (for June 1940) records her puzzlement at receiving no reply to a letter and a card dispatched to Clarence Terrace; when she telephoned, Elizabeth was out. Had someone been gossiping or making mischief? It wasn't, she decided, at all a trivial matter: 'for I was fond of her, and I think she of me . . .' The possibility of a break really gnaws at her over the next two days ('a slaty queasy feeling about E. B.'), and then she's soundly taking herself to task for jumping to conclusions. A letter has come from Elizabeth, friendly as ever: but still, no explanation for the silence.

By the mid 1930s certain young women, some with literary designs, were coming to regard Elizabeth in much the same way as Elizabeth regarded Virginia Woolf: with enthusiasm and deference. One such was the American poet and novelist May Sarton – 'that goose May Sarton', Virginia Woolf called her, having received from her the gift of a gentian. (She'd met the silly girl in Elizabeth's 'glass shining "contemporary" room', overlooking the lake.) May Sarton had first arrived at Clarence Terrace on a 'warm May evening', in 1936 (brought along, as a treat, by the author John Summerson). Elizabeth immediately put the goose in mind of a swan: 'stately, slightly awkward, beautiful and haunting' (these adjectives occur in her book of 1963, *I Knew a Phoenix*).

About Alan Cameron she's less enthusiastic, on this first occasion (she grew to like him later). He seemed the wrong husband for Elizabeth: a stout, red-faced, rather blimpish person with a walrus moustache. It was only when she'd recognized his kindness and loyalty to his wife that she was won over. Once, he took her to the nearby zoo, and she recounts how the pair of them went round peering into 'the grave and beautiful faces of leopards and lions and even tigers', looking for the one closest in appearance to Elizabeth. May Sarton is very free with her animal comparisons. John Summerson gets for his descriptive tag 'a shy heron', and Virginia Woolf is spotted looking not unlike a giraffe.

May Sarton stayed at Clarence Terrace in 1936 and recalls – in her autobiography, *A World of Light: Portraits and Celebrations* – Elizabeth, stretched out on a sofa, late at night, smoking a last cigarette after the departure of her dinner guests, and confiding to her young American admirer some details of her life. May Sarton, it seems, was told about Elizabeth's current love-affairs, and how they didn't interfere with her marriage to Alan. She, meanwhile, noted with appreciation Elizabeth's 'red-gold hair, pulled straight back into a loose knot at her neck', pale blue eyes (John Lehmann has said they were pale green) and 'awkwardly large hands', one often holding a cigarette in the air, weighed down by heavy bracelets. (Elizabeth's somewhat unexpected taste for showy jewellery impressed itself on many of her contemporaries.)

One love-affair which came to nothing was scheduled for the summer of 1936. (Victoria Glendinning tells the story in her biography.) A number of guests were expected at Bowen's Court, among them Goronwy Rees, a Welshman, ten years younger than Elizabeth, who had recently been appointed assistant editor of the *Spectator*. (Elizabeth first met him in Oxford, where he'd obtained a fellowship at All Souls in 1931.)

Elizabeth had reached Co. Cork in such a state of tiredness that she went to bed, stayed there for twenty-four hours and 'drank bromide'; then she kept losing her voice and could only croak or whisper. However, she was well enough to take driving lessons from Jim Gates (then manager of the creamery at Kildorerry, near Bowen's Court, and a life-long friend of Elizabeth's, just as his mother had been a friend of her mother's). She made good progress. 'I still feel rather terrified at intervals', she wrote to William Plomer. 'But I think this tends to make me a safe driver, as I am not at all dashing, and take no chances whatever.' (Friends driven by her in the 1950s have a different story to tell, as we shall see.) 'The feeling of independence is certainly very nice. At present I love driving the car when *alone* in it, but a passenger rather rattles me.'

That wasn't all she had to rattle her. Guests had started arriving towards the end of August: the Cecils came on a fleeting visit; then Noreen Colley; then Roger Senhouse and Rosamond Lehmann. They were followed by Isaiah Berlin with two of his students, Stuart Hampshire and Con O'Neill. Still others came. Then Goronwy Rees – and instead of the expected liaison with Elizabeth, an alliance was promptly formed between him and Rosamond Lehmann. It was, for these two, a matter of seizing the day.

Rosamond Lehmann, whose second marriage was in the course of breaking up, lived with her two children at Ipsden, near Oxford; Elizabeth had known her for some time. Between the loveliness of her appearance, and her talent for a kind of bitter-sweet writing, she was very much a romantic figure. The emotions of a decent woman inexpediently in love, and of the same character, younger, and excited by the prospect of a ball, are pungently expressed in two Lehmann novels of the 1930s, *Invitation to the Waltz* and its 1936 sequel, *The Weather in the Streets*.

Because of the way the bedrooms were arranged at Bowen's Court, Noreen Colley understood what was going on before Elizabeth did, and was outraged on her cousin's behalf. It wasn't a proper way for guests to carry on under Elizabeth's roof. As for Elizabeth – well, naturally she felt neglected and disgruntled, but put an extraordinarily good face on it ('Rosamond looked quite lovely, was sweet and I think enjoyed herself,' she wrote later to a friend). It wasn't a part of her disposition to show herself at a disadvantage. She wasn't a complainer, or a person who blurts out her grievances. Her instinct for hospitality triumphed over any chagrin she might have felt, though apparently she couldn't resist needling Goronwy Rees slightly when he stayed on with her and Noreen after everyone else had left – everyone including Alan, who'd been on the spot throughout the episode, as impassive as ever.

The business didn't stop rankling all at once. 'Life in general was rather getting me down,' Elizabeth wrote to William Plomer, apologizing for being poor company the last time they'd met, shortly after her return to England. (William Plomer had lent her a carpet – he wasn't sufficiently settled at this time to need it himself – and she was proposing to lay it in her own room.) She told him she'd just had four heavenly days in France, near Paris, which she spent being 'rather social and feminine', meeting some 'terrifying, upper-class, Proustian women', and attending an inferior drama about Queen Elizabeth. Clearly she was in good spirits again. Victoria Glendinning tells us that a slight awkwardness ensued between Elizabeth and Rosamond Lehmann (as well it might); though later, 'They were close again – closer than ever.' (Interesting that it was at Clarence Terrace that Rosamond Lehmann met Cecil Day Lewis, with whom she was entangled throughout the forties.)

Victoria Glendinning quotes an observation of Elizabeth's which seems characteristic: 'One wants to say,' she remarked, apropos men and their ways, 'break my heart if you must, but don't waste my time.' No one can say that her brush with Goronwy Rees was a waste of time: he turns up in *The Death of the Heart*, in the character of Eddie, who 'has to get off with people because he can't get on with them'. Goronwy Rees, we're to understand, was first charmed with the portrait, then took another look and became enraged; he thought of starting legal proceedings, but allowed himself to be dissuaded (notably by E. M. Forster, Victoria Glendinning says).

Eddie, in the novel, is taken up by Anna Quayne, an urbane woman in her mid-thirties who inhabits a house overlooking the lake at Regent's Park, has no children, a husband who sometimes resents the demands on his wife's time made by others (notably callers who hang their hats in the hall) and the present custody of his half-sister, product of an irregular and ludicrous union, now an orphan. Portia, her name is. Portia is sixteen and pure in heart. She's the quintessential Bowen innocent, for whom the ways of the world are painful and baffling. She isn't one for making adjustments in her scheme of values in order to get by.

Anna cannot take Portia to her somewhat vitiated heart. 'Either this girl or I are mad,' she declares to her writer friend St Quentin Miller (annoyance having sent her grammar haywire), in the famous opening scene of the book, with its view of frosty Regency terraces looming in the January dusk. There the two stand, on a frozen footbridge, well wrapped in cloth and fur, considering Portia's oddness – though St Quentin is really more concerned about his tea. What has happened? A diary kept by Portia has come into Anna's hands; and Anna is dismayed by its ingenuous appraisal of her actions. 'So I am with them, in London,' it starts; and continues trustfully.

Portia's trustfulness – she would even have trusted Anna not to read the diary – causes more than one character to convict her of utter lunacy. The story goes on: Portia meets Eddie, 'brilliant child of an obscure home', who has to play-act to advance himself (Anna, entertained by his antics, has got him a position with her husband's advertising firm, for which favour he isn't suitably grateful: there's a prickly side to Eddie, and his capriciousness may turn sour at any moment). 'He was like a bright little cracker that, pulled hard enough, goes off with a loud bang.' (The one thing dreaded by Elizabeth at childhood parties, we remember, was pulling crackers.) Portia falls in love with Eddie, who, in turn, sees in her the fullest reflection of his own all but reliquished innocence. She lends him her diary to read.

In the middle section of the novel, Portia is packed off to Seale-on-Sea, on the Kentish coast, to stay with Anna's old governess Mrs Heccomb, and her off-hand stepchildren, at a villa named Waikiki. (The seaside villas that enchanted the eight-year-old, we may note, have become a fit subject for satirical treatment.) Portia, to whom it occurs to invite her perfect Eddie to join her for a day or two – having received permission from her hostess to do so – is a bit of an odd fish among the jolly boys and girls of Seale-on-Sea, with their dances and gramophone records and lipsticks and outings along the beach. Eddie duly arrives and ingratiates himself with everyone, and especially with Daphne Heccomb, breezy daughter of Waikiki. We are next asked to consider poor Portia's distress and bewilderment, in a cinema, on observing that Eddie's right hand, which is holding hers, seems not to know what his left is up to. It is, in fact, entwined with the hand of Daphne Heccomb, who is seated on that side of him.

Portia cannot get things straight after this betrayal; Daphne, asked by Portia for an explanation, rounds on her with the news that she is insane. Eddie, similarly challenged, can only warn her against himself, explaining that he simply isn't available for the kind of exclusive or whole-hearted relationship she has in mind. Portia returns to Regent's Park. Then there is the business of the diary. Who has spoken about it to whom? St Quentin Miller, meeting Portia in the street, breaks it to her that her innermost thoughts aren't unknown to Anna. Did Eddie . . .? Eddie, when asked, says as a matter of fact it was Anna who mentioned Portia's diary to him, before Portia had so charmingly handed it to him for light reading. Portia, feeling laughed at behind her back, runs off to a fellow-sufferer – an old buffer called Major Brutt, who thinks of himself as a family friend of the Quaynes, but at whom they raise their eyebrows and poke mild fun. The distraught girl proceeds to enlighten the Major about the two-faced behaviour of his valued friends; not, we may be sure, out of anything akin to malice, but simply to make it clear to him – her last hope – that he and she are in the same boat. Why, in fact, should he not marry her? The next thing is a telephone call to 2, Windsor Terrace from the put-upon Major, demanding to be told how to handle this nuisance. The Quaynes are nonplussed for a minute or two, and then a simple solution strikes them: Matchett, Portia's ally, the old family servant who has no illusions about any of them, should be dispatched in a taxi to fetch the foolish girl. This is done.

As far as Elizabeth has put herself into the book at all – and there's always a danger of inferring too much from the real-life trappings, the house by the lake, the frequent callers, the childless marriage, etc. – she is split between Anna and Portia, and consequently unindulgent to both, which makes for vigour and astringency in the narrative. Though Portia may stand for candour, integrity and so forth, which can't but appeal to the right-minded, it is shown that the effect of such qualities is simply to get their possessor into various scrapes, which anyone with an ounce of knowingness might have avoided. (She is also, Elizabeth said, the archetypal unworldly girl who comes with her belongings in one pathetic trunk to stay with grand relations: somewhat in the position of the child Jane Eyre.) It is possible that the genesis of the book was in the author's own hurt feelings over the Goronwy Rees business (and she's reduced that episode to a marvellously trivial betrayal, a hand held heartlessly in a cinema), but if so, these feelings have been mocked, magnified and otherwise tampered with to the point of becoming irrelevant to the plan of the novel. Only the character of Eddie, as we have seen, remained sufficiently recognizable to annoy its prototype. (May Sarton has left a memorable picture of Alan Cameron, walking up and down the drawing-room at Clarence Terrace with a glass in his hand, reciting the first page of *The Death of the Heart*, and breaking off to shout, 'That's genius!')

Shortly before the house-party of 1936, Elizabeth mentioned to William Plomer the short-story collection, commissioned by T. S. Eliot, that she was putting together for Faber (it came out late in 1937), deploring the fad for hiker-narrators which had struck her in the course of her reading – 'As I crossed the horizon . . .': that sort of thing. Also, the artiness and mawkishness of so many stories were getting her down. So far, only *Midsummer Night's Madness*, by Seán O'Faoláin, had been a joy to read. 'Have you met him? Is he nice?' she wanted to know.

She soon had an opportunity to judge for herself. She and

Seán O'Faoláin, who'd been aware of one another since the early 1930s, finally met in the spring of 1937. He, born in Cork in 1900, was the son of a constable in the R.I.C., an ex-freedom fighter whose view of the Black and Tan war and the Civil War might be said to complement Elizabeth's 'big house' view, and a man of enormous erudition. He was born John Whelan, but preferred to use the Gaelic version of his name. In the summer of that year, he and Elizabeth went to Salzburg for the Festival, in a party which included Isaiah Berlin and Stuart Hampshire, and with the Connollys, togged up for mountaineering, putting in an appearance. Elizabeth's party, she says, were all either too small or too fat to follow suit in the matter of dress. 'Great fun' was had by everyone, and a piece on the Festival was written by Elizabeth for the short-lived magazine *Night and Day* (whose regular theatre reviewer she was). Mid-August found her at Bowen's Court, where she had a heavenly time reading Henri de Montherlant, and enjoyed the company of Raymond Mortimer and the Cecils. By the beginning of October she'd returned to London, to get on with her 'theatre job' for *Night and Day*.

'How I shall miss your theatre criticism,' Graham Greene wrote to her from Mexico, after the magazine had come to grief over a libel action brought on behalf of Shirley Temple, to whom he'd alluded injudiciously in a review. (The magazine's whole life-span had only been six months.) Elizabeth went on contributing to such periodicals as the *New Statesman*, the *Spectator*, *The Times Literary Supplement*, the *Observer*, *Vogue*, *Harper's Bazaar*, the *Tatler*, and Seán O'Faoláin's *The Bell* (for which, in 1942, she wrote an animated, slightly defensive essay on the big house, claiming credit for the Anglo-Irish, for the quality they'd added to Irish life), though she didn't especially enjoy reviewing, and, moreover, was reluctant to write about any book that she couldn't praise. A natural courteousness probably contributed to this stance, and also, perhaps, an idea that to ridicule inferior work in print was an unbecoming way of making one's mark.

Elizabeth saw something of Seán O'Faoláin when she visited Ireland in the early summer of 1938: five days in Dublin, and then Bowen's Court. In Dublin, she spent an evening with Yeats, 'who was an angel', at his home; and admired his 'superb white cat'. She also had a jolly day with Frank O'Connor (then living in Wicklow) – 'the most contemporary (I mean the least up-in-the-air) of the younger Irish, at least to talk to, I think.' Then it was Bowen's Court, where Tony Butts, a friend of William Plomer's, was due to paint her portrait. Soon she's reporting to William Plomer that the portrait is flying ahead: 'I must say, I do think it's a first-rate piece of work ... It also seems to me flattering, but no sitter, of course, minds that.' Her novel, *The Death of the Heart*, was also flying ahead: 'I'm now finishing the chapter-before-last, and hope to finish the last before I leave here.'

At a tea-party in 1938, Hugh Walpole came face to face with Elizabeth, 'dressed very smartly with a hat like an inverted coal scuttle', and thanked God that she and Virginia Woolf no longer frightened the life out of him, as they used to do. How intimidating was she? There's no doubt that her manner was grand, on occasion, that she made no bones about repelling over-familiarity, or that she could be caustic when the mood took her. Affected or dumb young girls, for instance, often drew a sharp comment from Elizabeth. 'Girls like that are brought along at owner's risk,' she said once, after a party, when a friend seemed concerned that a girl who'd hardly opened her mouth all evening might not have had a nice time. And of course anything 'claggy' (her word for the soggy, sentimental or flaccid) affronted her.

The thirties (Elizabeth's and the century's) were drawing to a close, and with them the literary world of *entre deux guerres* – Bloomsbury, the *New Signatures* poets, the inventors of parables, the documentary writers: those whose writing reflects contemporary history, and those who wrote to affect it – who wished, for example, to add a strong dash of communism to the English liberal spirit. War was very much in the air, especially after the Munich Agreement of September 1938; it was felt that the appeasers would ultimately go to the wall. There was ominous activity everywhere. 'Hitler yells on the wireless,' Louis MacNeice wrote in his *Autumn Journal* for 1938:

> The night is damp and still
> And I hear dull blows on wood outside my window;
> They are cutting down the trees on Primrose Hill . . .

The summit of Primrose Hill 'once was used for a gun emplacement/And very likely will/Be used that way again . . .' A kind of 'nervous irritability that has in it the pulse of our time', was singled out by Stevie Smith in her novel *Over the Frontier* (1938). And Elizabeth, reviewing C. Day Lewis's *Overtures to Death* in *Now and Then* (Winter 1938), wrote that the poems in this collection had 'a poetic relevance to all time, and are at the same time relevant to our perplexing day'.

Our perplexing day. Virginia Woolf, in a lecture delivered in May 1940 to the Workers' Educational Association, entitled 'The Leaning Tower', attributed to the conditions prevailing throughout the decade – disorder, malaise and a sense of the impending abolition of class – the failure of the 'thirties generation to achieve greatness in the poems, plays or novels they produced'. (It's a view, of course, that has often been disputed.) Elizabeth, who read a transcript of this talk on the train coming back to London after a visit to Rodmell, said later that the 'leaning tower' metaphor (standing for the writer bolstered up by money, social position and so forth, all of which were beginning to topple) seemed to her perfect. 'The quotations were damning', – and Virginia, she thought, not over-severe.

At the start of 1939 we find Elizabeth, hardly ever seen without a cigarette between her fingers, thanking Virginia Woolf (another inveterate smoker) for her Christmas present:

The perfectly lovely cigarette-holder, anti-nicotine, arrived just after Christmas, and I *do* thank you for it: I don't feel nearly so brown inside as I did, and I love smoking with it, also. It gives smoking an air, instead of making me feel like James Cagney, if you have seen him.

She goes on to say that they hadn't been able to get over to Ireland that Christmas, due to flu: flu which had a 'series of epilogues', including face-ache ('very undistinguished'). Domestic troubles piled up on her: her own flu, Alan's, the cook-general's poisoned thumb and the consequent deterioration of their diet ('cook very poisoned and so we do not have much food'). Fortunately her sense of humour did not fail her in the face of all this.

She mentions a pair of stockings she borrowed from Virginia Woolf on a day when they visited the Caledonian Market, and promises to return them. And she has a favour to ask:

A friend of mine from Ireland called Seán O'Faoláin wants to meet you so very much. I feel apologetic about people wanting to meet you, but he is a very nice young man, and a very good writer of short stories ... May I bring him to see you one day? I wouldn't ask if he were not very nice.

A meeting was duly arranged for the end of January, and then put off until 8 February, when Elizabeth took her Irish friend along to Tavistock Square. Virginia Woolf had received, that morning, a ring-casket from the estate of Lady Ottoline Morrell, who had died the previous April. 'The foreheads of the two women almost touched as they bent over the little casket to inhale the undying scent of its little, pale-green velvet cleft.' So Seán O'Faoláin, writing in the *London Review of Books* in 1982, remembered the occasion. He goes on,

Their two profiles, Virgina's exquisitely, delicately beautiful, Elizabeth's not beautiful but handsome and stately, were, as I recall them now, forty-four years after, like two young faces on an obsolete coin. Within months their world was under fire. Within half a dozen years it was dotted by ruins. Today we think of that pre-war world as an anachronism – until we read Woolf, or Forster, or Bowen, or Lehmann, or Waugh ...

In January 1939 Yeats had died ('He disappeared in the dead of winter,' Auden wrote); in the same month Eliot's *Criterion* came to an end. (Other literary periodicals, including *New Verse*, followed suit.) By the end of February the Spanish Civil War was over, and Virginia Woolf was writing to Elizabeth, on behalf of her niece Angelica Bell, to ask if the Clarence Terrace house might be borrowed for three days by the Artists' Committee for the Spanish Relief. Elizabeth and Alan agreed, but in the meantime the Committee had found another venue ('There was no need to bother you . . . I think you are amazingly generous. Yours – in a rush – V.') So, no function took place at Clarence Terrace that spring, apart from the annual tea-party given by Elizabeth and one of her aunts for Anglo-Irish old ladies.

Many things were coming to an end, and people – Elizabeth among them – were bracing themselves to meet the expected onslaught. In March 1939 German troops invaded Czechoslovakia; Chamberlain's appeasement policy was jettisoned when England and France agreed to stand behind Poland; later in the year, the Russo-German pact took some of the savour out of communism for certain English ideologues. Ordinary life continued in an atmosphere of edginess and hopes for a retrieval of nerve. Elizabeth, writing to William Plomer in August 1939, puts 'war-fears' among the causes of the state of tension and gloom – as it seems to her – afflicting her old friend Humphry House.

She is writing from Bowen's Court, having just dashed up to the Scottish Highlands, 'a fantastic expedition', for a wedding, and now, with Alan, enjoying 'the annual let-up': sleeping, yawning and droning around the fields. She hopes to be there until October, getting on with her book: her family history, entitled *Bowen's Court*, which became pretty well a history of Anglo-Ireland too. So it must have been on the Bowen's Court wireless, in neutral Ireland, that she heard the expected announcement of war, the king's speech and all the rest of it. The coming autumn proved to be a particularly lovely one, 'with colours such as I've never seen, and the country round here melting in light'. And certain improvements were carried out at Bowen's Court as planned: a telephone installed, and the house wired for electricity. Jim Gates (Elizabeth tells William Plomer), 'is busy putting in electric light for me here ... easier to work by than candles jumping about.' You could call it the end of an era.

SIX

'I want so much to do something at the moment, but ...
cannot *find* anything to catch hold of to *do*,' Elizabeth had
written to Virginia Woolf at the start of 1939, in a frustrated
postscript to a letter, at the same time asking to be told
Leonard Woolf's opinion of Sir Stafford Cripps. Clearly, she
had some sympathy with the idea of a 'Popular Front' to
oppose appeasement, as well as being anxious to involve
herself in national affairs. Whether or not she threw herself
behind that particular Labour MP, his objective was pretty
soon obtained.

Once war had broken out, Elizabeth became an ARP
warden, taking her turn at manning her local wardens'
post, answering inquiries from the public, and stomping up
and down the streets in dark-blue, official slacks, tin helmet
and boots, on the alert for black-out defaulters. Did she sit
like Connie, in *The Heat of the Day*, 'watching the hands of
the post clock go round and round, night in, day out, above
Mr Churchill's picture'? By all accounts, she was a very
plucky air-raid warden, once the blitz got under way; but
the 'Phoney War' period she may well have found trying.

Being an air-raid warden, however, wasn't Elizabeth's only wartime occupation. She was keen that her abilities should be used to the fullest extent in this time of crisis; and it occurred to her that there was work to be done in Ireland. Might she not draft a series of reports on the mood of the Irish, with regard to the war, also touching on more specific issues? There was, above all, the question of Irish ports being used by the British as refuelling stations. With due diffidence, she put her proposal to the Ministry of Information – and it was accepted. 'Now it's come to the point,' she told Virginia Woolf,

I have rather a feeling of dismay and of not wanting to leave this country. I am to see Harold Nicolson on Thursday and go to Ireland on Friday night next. I shall be at Bowen's Court first but I expect they will also want me to move about the place . . . I hope I shall be some good; I do feel it's important . . . It will all mean endless talk, but sorting out talk into shape might be interesting, I suppose.

She goes on to remark that Ireland can be dementing, if one is Irish; and will probably be so now. And she hopes that, if the country's to be invaded, this may take place while she is there: not a frivolous hope, she insists; just part of an honourable reluctance to shirk any danger that's going. '. . . If anything happens to England while I'm in Ireland I shall wish I'd never left, even for this short time.'

England at war claimed Elizabeth's allegiance absolutely, but she never, for a moment, ceased to think of herself as Irish. No amount of flitting about between England, Ireland and the Continent could dilute her sense of nationality – 'a

Top left: Henry Cole Bowen. *Top right:* Florence Bowen
Below: Elizabeth learning not to be a muff. Her mother and an old family groom are looking on

Above: Elizabeth as a young woman in the dining room at Bowen's Court
Left: Same period: the writer at work

Elizabeth drawn by Mervyn Peake

The Camerons snapped at Bowen's Court

In the library at Bowen's Court, 1947: a gathering of friends. Jim Gates is standing in the middle

Above: Bowen's Court
Left: Elizabeth regarding some
odd-looking pieces of sculpture
in the grounds at Bowen's Court.
(She called them 'the Uglies')

Above: 2, Clarence Terrace, Regent's Park: the Camerons' London home, photographed in 1945

Left: Alan Cameron lighting a cigarette

Below: On the back of this snapshot Elizabeth has written: 'Cat with kittens – me and some of the "creative writing" students at Seattle (University of Washington). The brunette beside me, wearing the white rose, is a little hell-cat: she wrote *the* most *brilliant* story!'

!957: Elizabeth with some Kildorerry neighbours

At a christening party for the Connollys' son. Elizabeth in conversation with Cyril
Connolly, Joy Craig and Caroline Blackwood

A formal portrait by Cecil Beaton

highly disturbing emotion', she called it in an interview published in *The Bell* in 1942; and added, 'It's not – I must emphasize – sentimentality.' Indeed: we know how she was affected by anything claggy. What she felt for Ireland was too pungent, on the one hand, and too disabused, on the other, to admit of any suspect strain. As for her position in the country – well, it has often been said that the fate of the Anglo-Irish is to be deemed Irish in England, and English in Ireland, the second sometimes carrying that slight inflection of hostility and irony that Elizabeth noted in the tone of 'big', as in the phrase 'big house', when uttered by a native. Of course, the equivocal always rivets the attention – we remember Browning's lines: 'Our interest's on the dangerous edge of things,/The honest thief, the tender murderer/The superstitious atheist . . .' (lines which Graham Greene has claimed could stand as epigraphs to all his books) and we might add, the English Irishwoman. Ambivalence was certainly a productive factor in the novelist's constitution. But in the conditions prevailing in Dublin in 1940, it was predominantly a cause of aggravation.

'The childishness and obtuseness of this country [Ireland] cannot fail to be irritating to the English mind,' Elizabeth announced in one of her undercover reports to Lord Cranborne at the Ministry of Information. The enormity of the current situation, she felt, ought to have prompted the Irish nation to jettison its long-standing grievances; however, 'there seems . . . only one basis on which Eire would consider treating for the ports. That is, on some suggestion from the British side that the Partition question was at least likely to be reconsidered . . .' Support for Britain, and sympathy for the British cause, was a fluctuating ethic in neutral Ireland: one minute in the ascendant, the next on the wane. It was apt to evaporate at any suggestion that Britain might try to requisition the ports. Eire, Elizabeth said, had invested its self-respect in its neutrality. The republic was making a stand, and meant to stick by it. It was also unwilling to expose itself to the threat of German bombing. Elizabeth didn't have very much sympathy with this attitude, which smacked to her of the unheroic; but neither did she admit the charge of 'disloyalty' when it was levelled against the Irish: 'given the plain facts of history', she says, the word simply isn't applicable. 'I could wish that the English kept history in mind more, that the Irish kept it in mind less.'

All the above information, and a good deal more, was gleaned by Elizabeth in the course of conversations she conducted in Dublin. She had taken a two-room flat overlooking Stephen's Green, when she arrived in Ireland in the summer of 1940, for the purpose of her 'activities'. From this base she went out to parties, some of them not very exhilarating, looked up old friends, who gave her tea or sherry, and noticed a decrease in realism of outlook, engendered by the wish to steer clear of the war. 'In Dublin I get engaged in deep, rather futile talks; it is hard to remember the drift afterwards, though I remember the words. I suppose that (smoke-screen use of words) is a trick of the Irish mind,' she wrote to Virginia Woolf. 'They are very religious. It is the political people I see mostly: it seems a craggy, dangerous, miniature world.' That was all she felt able to say about it in a letter; but she would like to talk, 'very much'.

She also noticed in Dublin that year a new enthusiasm for the Irish language and Irish culture, which struck her as being something of a declaration of distinctiveness, a separation from England and her concerns. She saw people got up in Irish national dress in the Dublin streets, and noted, 'Even the *Irish Times* now prints part of itself in Irish.' It was a development that left her cold.

A travel permit issued by the Ministry of Information enabled her to come and go between the two countries; otherwise, she'd have been cut off from Bowen's Court. During September and early October 1940 she was back in London, 'in a stupefied, excited and I think rather vulgar state', as she recalled it. The blitz had started. On the night of the first raids, in September, a thousand people died in London. The docks were burned. Many homes were reduced to rubble – the Woolfs' at Mecklenburgh Square was severely damaged. 'When your flat went did that mean all the things in it too?' Elizabeth asked in a letter. 'All my life I have said, "Whatever happens there will always be tables and chairs" – and what a mistake.' She also wondered, 'Were all those streets that were burnt the streets we walked about?' That walk, through the Temple, along the river, up Thames Street, to the Tower, had taken place in the summer, and included a lot of talk about Elizabeth's government mission in Ireland, and Virginia's 'greatness'.

At the end of June 1940 Elizabeth had spent two idyllic days with the Woolfs at their Sussex home at Rodmell, came away bearing a cactus plant and garlic, and thought, in retrospect, that she had never been 'so perfectly happy' as she was during that brief visit. 'I loved everything we did.' (This included shredding redcurrants in a room at the top of the house.) Virginia Woolf, you might say, furnished an outlet for whatever effusiveness existed in Elizabeth's nature. ('If I began to write about affection for you, Virginia, I should degenerate into sheer gush.')

For the whole of one week in September 1940 Elizabeth and Alan were cut off from Clarence Terrace on account of a time-bomb just inside the gates of Regent's Park. (Elizabeth has described the experience in her essay, 'London 1940', included in her *Collected Impressions*.) Installed, with a lot of other people in the same predicament, in an Oxford Street hotel, they were promptly threatened by another un-exploded bomb. 'It has been a dirty night.' Alan – who had joined the Home Guard, and been made responsible for the defence of Broadcasting House during air raids – took control of things, organized the removal of everyone from the danger zone, some with pyjama legs showing below their overcoats, and then went to stand in the roadway, wearing a tin hat and L.D.V. armlet, to direct the traffic. Elizabeth noted the splinters of glass among the fallen leaves, the mousy dust shed by ruined buildings, 'as bodies shed blood'. 'The violent destruction of solid things,' she has written elsewhere, '. . . left all of us, equally, heady and disembodied.'

Among those who stuck it out in London were people 'whom the climate of danger suited' (as we read in *The Heat of the Day*), who found themselves exhilarated, as well as disorientated, by the blitz. A slight contempt for the bolters, and consequent camaraderie among themselves, helped to make things tolerable for the stayers-on, subjected nightly as they were to sleeplessness and fear. An unaccustomed emptiness was discernible in many London squares and terraces, while other parts of the country seemed 'unnaturally full'. Town houses, some with weakened structures, were shut or boarded up. By the beginning of 1941, in Clarence Terrace, only one other house apart from the Camerons' was occupied: 'A house with a *reputation*,' Elizabeth said, 'full of rather gaudy, silent young men who come out in the mornings and walk about two and two, like nuns.'

Later in the autumn of 1940 Elizabeth crossed to Ireland again, and one afternoon in November she took tea in Dublin with a prominent opponent of Irish neutrality, James Dillon, the Fine Gael deputy leader, who was adamant in his opinion about the justness of the Allied cause. Elizabeth, on the alert for anything that might influence Irish opinions in general, was struck by Dillon's political astuteness, and also by the mixture of worldly and monkish elements in his personality; in one of her dispatches she alludes to his 'deep religious fanaticism'. (Many years later, after her death, when he was shown a copy of this dispatch, Dillon was affronted by the way Elizabeth had abused his hospitality, back in 1940, by writing up what he'd taken to be a private conversation. As for the 'religious fanaticism' she'd attributed to him, 'Poor woman – you can see her unhappy agnosticism,' he said. It's an odd verdict on a frequent church-goer and unostentatious Protestant.)

Elizabeth picked up an impression of Catholic self-righteousness in Ireland's attitude to the war, which was held to be a judgement on England for her atheism and materialism. Anything that smacked of Communist Russia, even the word 'revolutionary', as in, 'We younger people in Britain are fighting this as a revolutionary war,' was apt not to go down too well in Catholic circles. (One would have thought that the Irish connotations of the word were strong enough to blot out others.) The Irish were inclined to credit themselves with a spiritual approach to living, and to see their escape from the worldwide conflict as an outcome of this trait.

Christmas, as usual, was spent at Bowen's Court in the second winter of the war, in freezing weather, with the house very cold and empty, and 'very beautiful in a glassy sort of way'. There were some early lambs, which Elizabeth envisaged breaking through the fence and coming to bleat on the frosty lawn beneath her windows. She read Maupassant, noting his 'sharp senses but really rather boring mind'. Alan returned to London early in the new year, while Elizabeth stayed on until the end of the month to finish *Bowen's Court*.

Because of her restless and strung-up state she didn't, for once, enjoy being there on her own, and found it difficult to write letters or make plans. In the absence of petrol for the car, she wished she had a riding horse. A bicycle was the best she could manage – however, 'I keep wanting to get off and sit on the bank to smoke and think and cheer up.' On the bicycle, she rode to Mitchelstown, 'a beautifully planned but sad little town up under the Galtee mountains', to visit her aunt, Sarah Bowen, who lived there in rooms in the square.

She craved companionship, but quarrelled with her old

Kildorerry friend Jim Gates, whom for some reason she accused of utter stupidity before calming down and repenting of the outburst. 'I have been cruel to Mr Gates because I made the mistake I so often make, of idealizing at the outset a stupid person.' This seems, on the face of it, an odd rationalization. Lifelong acquaintance with Jim Gates, one would have thought, would have kept Elizabeth from forming any illusions about his character. Was it Ireland's neutrality that caused the row? In any case, the breach wasn't final. The friendship was too deeply rooted to be broken by heated words, and moreover, Jim Gates was one of the masculine, unliterary men who satisfied some robust element in Elizabeth's nature: 'a big, fair, smiling, offhand' man, whose 'manner with women was easy and teasing, but abstract and perfectly automatic'. These words describe Robinson, in the story 'Summer Night', for whom – Victoria Glendinning tells us – Jim Gates supplied a starting-off point. (Only a starting-off point; the relationship described in the story doesn't in the least resemble that between Elizabeth and Jim Gates.)

Robinson is a factory manager in an Irish town; in the story, he is calmly awaiting the arrival of an excited woman, and, at the same time, acting sociably towards a pair of chance visitors, a brother and sister, one rather tiresome and effete, the other stone deaf. Emma, a woman married to a Major, who is driving sixty miles through the night to keep an illicit tryst with Robinson, is defeated by her lover's pragmatism when she reaches him bearing her whole-heartedness as a gift. She thinks for a moment that he has broken her heart, but really it is only her fairy tale that's been demolished. Elizabeth, once again, is at the business of shattering romance at the same time as evoking it.

Elizabeth was very anxious to know Virginia Woolf's opinion of this story, which went into her 1941 collection, *Look at All Those Roses*. Other pieces in the book, she said, had been written three, four or five years earlier, and now impressed her as being 'rather *shrewish*'. It's not a fair comment; the title story, for example, reminds us how striking her use of atmosphere can be; and the fact that it's cut short at the most tantalizing moment adds greatly to the power of the narrative. Irish asperity, too, gets a showing when we are told of Lou, the central character, that 'her idea of love was adhesiveness'. But clearly, 'Summer Night', as the most recent thing she'd done, was at the forefront of her mind. Or else she uses the word 'shrewish' tentatively hoping to be contradicted; we don't know if this object was achieved.

Probably her book was among the topics discussed during her second visit to Rodmell, which took place in the middle of February, and, like the earlier visit, filled her with happiness: 'hope happiness didn't make me too bouncing', she said in her thank-you letter. She'd come away enchanted by the memory of an upper room at Monk's House, Rodmell, complete with cyclamens and arum lilies, and Virginia's embroidery – and of Virginia herself, suddenly throwing back her head and hooting with laughter, in the middle of mending a torn curtain.

This letter – as it turned out, the last she ever wrote to Virginia Woolf, who was dead before the following month was out – contains descriptions of visits to the War Office and the Dominions Office, on business relating to Ireland.

At the former, she'd been intrigued to find everyone drinking glasses of milk (it was eleven in the morning), which somehow didn't fit in with her image of the place.

Lord Cranborne, at the Dominions Office, was David Cecil's brother; and Elizabeth had asked to be put in touch with him because, 'I knew he had seen the reports I'd been sending in, and there were things I wanted to say that I couldn't write.' An appointment was duly arranged, but getting into the Dominions Office proved a thorny business. She didn't know where the building was, and aroused suspicion by arriving in a taxi. A number of obstacles then had to be surmounted: men with bayonets, the filling in of forms, long passages to be negotiated. Finally she reached a room with a Turkey carpet and roaring fire, and received a full measure of 'sympathetic and charming Cecil politeness'. It wasn't just a show – Lord Cranborne had been so impressed by a report she'd sent in the previous November that he promptly passed it on to the Foreign Office for Lord Halifax's personal attention. He was particularly taken with Elizabeth's 'shrewd appreciation' of the state of things in Ireland. (The enterprising decision to make use, for political ends, of a novelist's antennae, had clearly paid off, as far as everyone was concerned.)

In her previous letter to Virginia Woolf, written just after her return from Ireland at the beginning of February, Elizabeth mentions an engagement she has at Elsfield. Billy Buchan's daughter was being christened – 'that little Billy Buchan who used to live with us: it seems very odd his having a daughter at all' – and Elizabeth had agreed to act as godmother to the child. A fellow-guest at the Buchan christening party (champagne, and pink marzipan sweets served in white Sèvres bonbonnières) was Charles Ritchie, a debonair Canadian diplomat (born in 1906) who spent the war years in London. An entry in Charles Ritchie's diary records his first encounter with Elizabeth, singling out her good appearance, intelligent, handsome face and the watchfulness of her expression. Her alertness took Charles Ritchie by surprise; he'd been expecting someone more insouciantly Irish.

Later that year he confesses: 'The first time I saw Elizabeth Bowen I thought she looked more like a bridge-player than a poet.' (What *did* she look like? Rosamond Lehmann, writing to correct some misstatements in the *Times* obituary of Elizabeth Bowen in 1973, said that she was just above medium height – not 'very tall' at all – and always, before her last illness, seemed endowed with enviable health and stamina. At this point, in the early forties, she would have been in her prime.) This impression soon gave way, in Charles Ritchie's mind, to a sense of something 'mysterious, passionate and poetic', behind the urbane exterior. He also appreciated her dryness and humour, when he got to know her better. It didn't take long for the two to become friends. We don't know what impression Charles Ritchie made on Elizabeth straight away, but it was clearly favourable. ('At the first glance they saw in each other's faces a flash of promise, a background of mystery'; so she refers to Stella and Robert in *The Heat of the Day*.) Before long, he is dining at Clarence Terrace, where he is able to observe her talent for entertaining. She rings him at Canada House; they go together, 'on a perfect September afternoon', to view the roses at Regent's Park – a romantic excursion. 'As we walked together,' Charles Ritchie writes, 'I seemed to see the flowers through the lens of her sensibility. The whole scene, the misty river, the Regency villas with their walled gardens and damp lawns and the late September afternoon weather blended into a dream – a dream in which these were all symbols soaked with a mysterious associative power . . .'

'The very temper of pleasures lay in their chanciness, . . . in their being off-time,' Elizabeth wrote in *The Heat of the Day*. Anything might happen. On the inverse of enjoyment, Charles Ritchie noted in his diary after the bombing of the Café de Paris: '. . . that is about all there is to do – just curse and go home and wait to wake up the next morning to see what else is gone.'

One of the things Charles Ritchie liked about Elizabeth was her inability to sprawl, 'mentally or physically'. This observation is prompted by a visit she paid him, late in 1941, in the course of which she'd arranged herself elegantly on a sofa. She arrived wearing a smart black coat with a pink flower in the buttonhole, and took it off to disclose gold chains and bangles (which, on her, managed not to look flashy). On another occasion, dining at Clarence Terrace, Charles noticed that Elizabeth had on 'a necklace and bracelet of gold and red of the kind of glass that Christmas tree ornaments are made of' – a present from a woman friend who saw Elizabeth as 'a Byzantine type'.

The relationship flourished. There were outings to Hampstead and Kew, a lot of drifting through azaleas and rhododendrons in a dreamlike state, sheltering under a weeping willow when it suddenly rained, dining at Claridges, lunching at the Ritz, drinking a lot of red wine, social evenings, literary friends, conversations about writing. One Christmas morning they attended a service at Westminster Abbey, returning to Clarence Terrace to join Alan for lunch. At one point, in a different season, Charles lay on a sofa, looking out at a 'sea of green tree tops', while Elizabeth, 'in an excited way', regaled him with the plot of 'The Happy Autumn Fields'. (There were few people with whom she'd discuss her work – Virginia Woolf was one, Charles another.) By the middle of 1942, Charles was declaring, 'I now know that this attachment is nothing transient but will bind me as long as I live.'

The Anglo-Irishwoman and the Anglo-Canadian had certain affinities of temperament: gregariousness, incalculability and a special, non-native way of regarding England. 'Who could help becoming attached to her?' Charles wondered when he considered Elizabeth; she, undoubtedly, felt the same about him. Whenever she left for Ireland and her war-work, he missed her. One year, just before Christmas, they travelled to Wiltshire together to spend a weekend with Stephen Tennant, whose country house, all but one wing, had been taken over by the Red Cross. On the train, they found themselves sitting opposite Augustus John, and at Salisbury station their host met them wearing a blue knitted helmet. In the evening, Elizabeth gave her views on dialogue in the novel – how every sentence 'must bear directly or indirectly on the theme'. (Three years later, she reiterates this point in her 'Notes on Writing a Novel', published in *Orion II*: 'It [dialogue] must be pointed, intentional, relevant. It must crystallize situation. It must express character. It must advance plot.')

Two books of Elizabeth's which came out in 1942 were her family history, *Bowen's Court* (this book had been suggested by her agent Spencer Curtis Brown, while he was staying with her in Ireland in the late 1930s), and its offshoot, *Seven Winters*. (There was a third book in that year – *English Novelists*, in the Collins 'Britain in Pictures' series.) Between them, these books contain everything Elizabeth had to say on the subject of the Anglo-Irish: their lavishness, stylishness, aplomb, high-handedness and obtuseness. In *Bowen's Court*, we get an interesting account of historical events as they impinged on a particular group in Ireland – the gentry of northeast Co. Cork. The author's stance is humane and intelligent, her style inspired, and she shows throughout a kind of enlightened conservatism akin to Edmund Burke's (as Hermione Lee points out in her introduction to the Virago reissue of *Bowen's Court*). She isn't out to glorify her forebears, and others like them, but, as always, she means to see that they are given their due. On the charge of snobbishness, for instance – 'big house' people, she says (in her essay on 'The Big House'), 'admit only one class distinction: they instinctively "place" a person who makes a poor mouth'.

It wasn't only the Anglo-Irish who disparaged the cult of the poor mouth – which, 'in Gaelic and in Anglo-Irish dialect', simply means parading one's wretchedness in order to obtain charity. We don't know if Elizabeth, in Dublin, ever ran across Flann O'Brien, whose satirical Gaelic novel *An Béal Bocht* (*The Poor Mouth*) was published in 1941 (but not issued in an English translation until 1973). *An Béal Bocht* offers a devastatingly comic appraisal of Gaelic fatalism, hardship and self-satisfaction, written with as much verve and distinction as anyone could wish.

Elizabeth, who was at one with the poor (she said) in possessing a 'savage or animal distrust of hospitals', had to spend a week in a nursing home in Mandeville Place having 'wisdom and other refractory back teeth' extracted, an operation which took place 'at the gallows-like hour of 8.30 a.m.'. That done, she quickly regained her high spirits, and went about as smartly and animatedly as ever. John Lehmann, in his autobiography, conjuring up an archetypal literary party of the early 1940s, places Elizabeth at one end of a crowded room, has her discuss novels with Philip Toynbee, and makes things as lively and illustrious as can be with the names he adds to these two: Graham Greene, Henry Green, C. Day Lewis, Louis MacNeice, Henry Reed, Rosamond Lehmann, Rose Macaulay, Laurie Lee, William Plomer, Raymond Mortimer, Roger Senhouse, Veronica Wedgwood.

Clarence Terrace continued to be a centre of hospitality, the blitz notwithstanding. Stephen Spender remembers an instance of *sang-froid* as displayed by Elizabeth, who assembled her guests on the balcony overlooking Regent's Park, kept them there drinking coffee, without comment, throughout an air raid, and only remarked, as they went indoors, that she felt she ought to apologize for the noise. However, the blitz was a subject she couldn't avoid in ordinary conversation, and didn't want to; when she met James Lees Milne for the first time (at lunch with Margaret Jourdain and Ivy Compton-Burnett), she was happy to discuss with him the recent bombing of London, while he quickly modified his initial rather unfavourable impression of her (as a lot of people seem to have done). When she entered the room he saw her as ugly, 'with a prominent nose and a drop on the end of it'; however, when he looked again, she'd become handsome, 'but not beautiful'. Then he succumbed to her charm. 'I liked her.'

The Demon Lover and *The Heat of the Day* are among the handful of contemporary works of fiction that put their finger on some quintessential mood or flavour or set-up peculiar to the time. (In this respect they stand with Waugh's *Put Out More Flags*, with Graham Greene's *The Ministry of Fear*, and with the novels *Caught* and *Back* by Henry Green.) From the *Demon Lover* stories we learn exactly what it was to live in London through the blitz, to suffer dislocation and derangement of the senses, to see the city reshape itself more strangely every day, to attach importance to the acquisition of an egg, to be a woman unaccustomed to opening her own front door, the owner of a shut-up house, or a man revisiting a seaside promenade, now empty and derelict. Wartime conditions allow various accesses for the uncanny. Elizabeth, reading the proofs of the book, was struck by something she hadn't noticed before: 'a rising tide of hallucination', sweeping through the stories. In the last story of all, a moonlit, unearthly city ('Mysterious Kor') is superimposed over ordinary London. As a ghost story, 'The Demon Lover', ominous and relentless, is unsurpassable. (With this book, incidentally, Elizabeth moved from Gollancz to Cape, who remained her publisher from this point on. Her editor there was William

Plomer, back at his desk after his wartime stint with naval intelligence at the Admiralty.)

The stories were written between the spring of 1941 and the late autumn of 1944, one – 'The Happy Autumn Fields' – in a flat borrowed from Clarissa Churchill, while 2, Clarence Terrace was put in order after suffering bomb damage. The house had been blasted a number of times; finally the ceilings came down and the windows were shattered. They had to move out. 'The house rocked: simultaneously the calico window split and more ceiling fell . . . The enormous, dull sound of the explosion died, leaving a minor trickle of dissolution still to be heard in parts of the house.' This shaking-up is experienced by Mary, an overwrought woman in an endangered building, for whom a fragment of experience out of the past, transmitted to her in a hallucinatory way – a Victorian family in Co. Cork, two young sisters unnaturally close to one another, and an impending tragedy in the happy autumn fields – has blotted out the urgency of self-preservation.

There is an entry in Charles Ritchie's diary for April 1942 in which he recounts walking in Hampstead with Elizabeth, and listening to her talk about Virginia Woolf: the graceful figure she made, in some flowing dress of mauve or grey, her 'fairy cruelty', when she failed to understand how her words could hurt, how everyone fell under her spell, and how impossible it was to make sense of this to those who hadn't known her (for Charles Ritchie, her 'reflected atmosphere' remained 'rather alarming'). She was, Elizabeth said, 'one of the only two of the dead whom I *truly* miss' (the other being William Plomer's flamboyant friend Tony Butts, who died in 1941). News of her suicide had reached Elizabeth, at Bowen's Court, via someone who had heard it announced on the wireless. In the letter she sent at once to Leonard Woolf, she said: 'A great deal of the meaning seems to have gone out of the world.'

As early as January 1942 Elizabeth told Charles Ritchie that she would like to put him in a novel, adding, 'You probably would not recognize yourself.' The novel he went into is *The Heat of the Day* (dedicated to him), but it's by no means – in accordance with Elizabeth's usual practice – a straightforward portrayal. For one thing, Robert Kelway, the Charles Ritchie figure in the book, is a holder of aberrant views. This is a device by which Elizabeth extends her usual theme of betrayal to suit the wartime setting. Treason, no less than tension, is a by-product of the time.

The predicament of fastidious Stella Rodney, the novel's central character, is to find herself in love with a traitor. Robert is a Dunkirk-wounded man and secret Fascist. The truth about how things stand, in this respect, is divulged to Stella by the espionage agent who's been keeping tabs on Robert: the charmless, impassive and seedy Harrison. Harrison, the possessor of slightly asymmetrical eyes, cherishes an infelicitous hope of forming an attachment to Stella; and as a means of sexual persuasion he holds out the offer of freedom for Robert, for a time at least. What he's getting at isn't lost on Stella. 'Yes, I quite see,' she tells him. 'I'm to form a disagreeable association in order that a man may be left free to go on selling his country.'

This is a novel that contains many styles: lyrical, comical, evocative, plain, idiosyncratic. Elizabeth Bowen shows her mastery of each in turn. Stella's unease, and the wider unease it reflects, are at the core of the book. As Elizabeth herself said of Le Fanu's *Uncle Silas*, you have to submit to the author's 'hypnotizing' sense of – in this case – 'a particular psychic London', first during the 'heady autumn' of the earliest air raids, then in the dangerless September of 1942. It's easy to pick holes in the plot, to look in vain for practical espionage, to find vagueness where particularity seems called for, to accuse the author of creating an insubstantial traitor figure. There is something in these complaints, but they die away when the book is considered *in toto*, and its achievement acknowledged. It renders with the utmost keenness and subtlety the sights and sensations available in wartime.

This is the book, as well, in which Elizabeth succeeds in raising colloquial speech to a high level of stylization. (When she'd tried it before, in such lower-class monologues as 'Oh, Madam . . .' and 'Love', it hadn't come off, a plethora of 'did oughts' and 'ever so queers' in these pieces producing an effect of monotony.) Louie and Connie, in factory and ARP positions, are a couple of working-class girls who talk like this: 'Often you say the advantage I should be at if I could speak grammar; but it's not only that. Look at the trouble there is when I have to only say what I *can* say, and so cannot ever say what it is really . . . I could more bear it if I could only say.' It's Henry Green's trick of presenting the ordinary eccentrically, and, in Elizabeth's hands, it is very nearly as effective.

One girl – Louie – is saddled with abject naïveté, while the other has a managing disposition. Between them, these two supply much scope for robustness and comedy, as well as furthering the plot. It is Louie, for example, blundering into the wrong night-club in the black-out, who saves Stella from the consequences of her last-stake decision to sleep with the shady Harrison: Robert is beyond saving at this point. Robert's shadiness is another matter: it has more of the romantic about it. His character, in a sense, bears out Elizabeth's former proposition: that 'complex people are never certain that they are not crooks' (she has also left on record her fellow-feeling for the dark horse). A complex novelist, likewise, can never view anything straight-forwardly, neither an everyday betrayal nor an act of treachery in wartime. Too much intervenes between the topic and its presentation: the colouring of a mood, the author's whims, digressions, what-have-you. Elizabeth's oblique approach to her central ideas has often brought down on her the charge of evasiveness. (Oddly enough, 'straightforward' is the word she applied to *The Heat of the Day*: when William Plomer asked her to write a blurb, and she had difficulty in doing so, she declared that the novel was sufficiently straightforward not to need a blurb – 'Nothing about it really needs to be explained.')

It's not really a fair charge, and it was usually levelled by people exasperated by her work for other reasons: its middle-class bias, for example, or the mannerisms including periphrasis and sometimes ostentatious convolution. By the late 1940s the Bowen style was sufficiently recognizable to make a target for amiable mockery (there's a funny Bowen parody in a 1952 *New Yorker*). And, as Seán O'Faoláin has said, 'every critic has made fun of Elizabeth Bowen's swanky vocabulary'.

Rosamond Lehmann, who was bowled over by the *The Heat of the Day*, nevertheless put her finger on the most puzzling thing about it – that Robert's allegiance belonged to Nazi Germany rather than to Communist Russia. (This struck other people. Francis King, in his obituary of Elizabeth, had actually made the transference in his own mind: he refers to Robert as a *Communist* agent.) Elizabeth had been on the periphery of Communist-enthusiast circles in the 1930s: Maurice Bowra, for example, knew Guy Burgess, who, through him, became a friend of Goronwy Rees. (Burgess at one point actually tried to get Rees into the spying business alongside himself.) Rees was also a friend of Anthony Blunt. (These connections are all noted by Hermione Lee in her book on Elizabeth Bowen.) Something of all this must have been transmitted to Elizabeth, via gossip if nothing else; and it's likely that she'd have picked up the arguments of Communist ideologues among her acquaintances. She had, you might say, a ready-made brand of political delinquency at her disposal, something running counter to the feeling in the country (which she needed for her plot), yet less unpalatably deviant than a yen for Nazism. But she makes a Fascist of her character, and fails to be altogether convincing about how this ideology grew on him.

The Heat of the Day was a difficult book to write. 'It presents every possible problem in the world,' Elizabeth remarked to Charles Ritchie; and indeed it took a considerable time – at least five years – to get it knocked into shape. Having to live away from Clarence Terrace between July and October 1944 didn't help. In the midst of nervous strain and upheaval, 'she is still frantically trying to write her novel', Charles Ritchie noted in the passage in his diary which laments the mutilation of No. 2: 'It was the last house in London which still felt like a pre-war house.'

Elizabeth had already told Charles quite a lot about her method of working – how, for example, she overdid everything to start with, throwing in every descriptive word that came to mind, and going all out for a particular effect, then, 'cutting down and discarding and whittling away'. No doubt she got down to the novel with the relationship between herself and Charles Ritchie very much in mind, and then whittled it down, virtually, to the atmosphere in which it was conducted. A crucial and much-quoted passage in the novel underscores the point: 'But they were not alone, nor had they been from the start, from the start of love. Their time sat in the third place at their table. They were the creatures of history, whose coming together was of a nature possible in no other day – the day was inherent in the nature.'

Charles Ritchie was recalled to Ottawa at the start of 1945: 'I miss Elizabeth more and more,' he wrote in his diary a few months later. When work demanded his full attention he was able to banish her from his conscious mind, 'but now that I am idle thoughts of her besiege me'. Early in 1946 he was back in London, but only briefly: 'this miserable spy-ring affair removed any possible last chance of his prolonging his time in London', Elizabeth told William Plomer. (The case she mentions concerned the identification, via a recanting Soviet cipher clerk, of a number of Soviet agents, including a senior member of the British High Commission's Registry and the atomic scientist, Nunn May.)

On VE Day Elizabeth finished two commissioned pieces of work, had two guests to lunch, and went out in the evening to observe the victory celebrations, which included a bonfire at one end of Clarence Terrace, and many people milling about in a kind of daze of exaltation. 'I must say that I drank a good deal,' she said. Now that the war was over, it seemed to her a good moment to take stock: of herself, her plans, achievements, what the last few years had meant. She writes to Cyril Connolly, applauding the spirit he has kept in existence, through his periodical *Horizon*, and through something intangible connected with his presence about the place. She commends William Plomer for the way he has discharged his wartime duties at the Admiralty: efficiently and without fuss, unlike some people who have gone on about their 'interrupted lives'. In this letter she admits that she has had a good war, 'if you know what I mean. I cannot say I'm ashamed of the fact, as I don't think I had a good war at anybody else's expense, but it is a fact.' (Those who thrived in the dicey conditions of wartime were possessed, as Elizabeth was, of 'one kind of wealth: resilience'.)

She is writing this letter from Bowen's Court, where she arrived, 'full of irritations and repugnances': these got worked out of her system by means of outdoor activity, 'hewing down nettles and undergrowth, clearing woods'. It was just what she needed. Her plans, she said, were fluid; but it was strongly in her mind and Alan's that they should ship the bulk of their furniture from Clarence Terrace to Bowen's Court, and spend more time there. (Already they had sub-let the top floors at Clarence Terrace.) Alan, whose eyes were giving trouble (an effect of his trench poisoning in the First World War), had decided to retire from the BBC. In the event, it was only a partial retirement – he was employed by EMI, for example, as adviser on educational gramophone records, and he worked as an editor on the Oxford History of Music on Record.

As for Elizabeth, 'I've been coming gradually unstuck from England for a long time,' she confided to William Plomer. The only thing that had kept her attached to the country was Mr Churchill and the stylishness he conferred on it. 'I've always felt, "When Mr Churchill goes, I go."' And, in a rather uncharacteristic outburst, she proceeds to denounce 'all these little, middle-class, Labour wets with their old London School of Economics ties . . .' Post-war malaise? (The date of the letter is September 1945.) Perhaps her rather jaundiced outlook at this moment was due, in fact, to impending jaundice, to which she succumbed early in the new year, and which left her feeling 'very dopey and peculiar' until well into February. While in bed, she read and reread 'The Ancient Mariner', until she'd almost got it off by heart. When she recovered she was able to take an interest in the Paris hats which were starting to appear in London – 'disturbing us who have not yet got one'.

V. S. Pritchett and Graham Greene came to Clarence Terrace to discuss a proposed book consisting of an exchange of letters between the three of them (it was published by Percival Marshall in 1948 under the title *Why Do I Write?*). They talked about Henry James; V. S. Pritchett noted Elizabeth's 'lovely whistling stammer'. (In 1942, Charles Ritchie tells us, she'd gone to an Austrian psychoanalyst to have her stammer cured, but ended by telling him nothing at all about herself, while he told her the story of his life. The stammer stayed with her.) Elizabeth, in the book, offers 'one emotional reason why one may write': 'the need to work off, out of the system, the sense of being solitary and farouche'. And the last word falls to her, when she claims that writers, by *not* contributing to anarchy, contribute something to life in general.

Elizabeth was gaining public recognition: she was made a Companion of the British Empire, and was listed in *Who's Who*. Trinity College, Dublin, gave her an Honorary Litt. D. She employed a secretary, though Alan continued to look after her practical affairs. She did some lecture tours for the British Council, one covering Czechoslovakia and Austria, early in 1948. In Vienna, she was taken out to dinner by Graham Greene, who happened to be there at the same time. After dinner, at his suggestion, they went on to a seedy night-club where, he'd promised her, a police raid would take place at midnight. Elizabeth was impressed when this duly occurred, not realizing that her novelist friend had set up the incident to amuse her. (He tells the story in his autobiography *A Sort of Life*.) Later that year, Elizabeth tells William Plomer that she's about to leave for Paris, en route for Hungary, again at the behest of the British Council, who bungled the travel arrangements this time; there was some trouble over an out-of-date visa.

The years between 1946 and 1952 were eventful and interesting for Elizabeth, what with the restoration of trips abroad, as many meetings with Charles Ritchie as could be managed (some in Paris while he was attached to the Canadian Embassy there, at least one in Ottawa while she was lecturing in the States in 1951), increasing acclaim for her work and the consequent demands made on her, new departures such as her appointment (in 1949) to the Royal Commission on Capital Punishment, which reported its findings – pro-abolition – in 1953. John Lehmann, in his memoirs, recalls Henry Yorke (Henry Green) at a dinner party, subjecting Elizabeth to avid questioning about her capital punishment activities, 'in a way that managed to make even that macabre subject grotesquely amusing'.

The success of *The Heat of the Day* (published in 1949) enabled Elizabeth to have proper bathrooms installed at Bowen's Court; guests before this had had to make do with her grandfather Robert's water closets. Her books were reissued by Cape in a uniform edition around this time; and, in America, Knopf brought out a new edition of her earliest stories, for which she supplied an introduction. In collaboration with John Perry – who had also collaborated with her friend Molly Keane (M. J. Farrell) – she wrote a play with an Anglo-Irish theme, 'Castle Anna', which was staged at the Lyric, Hammersmith, after a provincial tour (it wasn't very successful). A book she'd undertaken on the Shelbourne Hotel in Dublin came out in 1951 (published by

Harrap). *The Shelbourne*, from its vantage point in the hotel itself, considers the character of Dublin in an engaging and distinctive way. A short critical study of her work – from which, she said, she learned a lot – was written by Jocelyn Brooke, and published by the British Council in 1952.

Elizabeth's social activities continued unabated too: we find her staying with the Day Lewises, acquiring another godchild in the Spenders' daughter Elizabeth, organizing gatherings of friends at Bowen's Court, just as in the pre-war days. The American novelist and short-story writer Eudora Welty, whom Elizabeth greatly admired and liked, came to stay a few times, on one occasion presenting her hostess with a porcelain drinking-chocolate-maker. The odd guest, however, proved a bit of a strain. One such was another American, Carson McCullers, who turned up boisterously in May 1950, wearing jeans and a multi-coloured coat, required constant amusement and, when it wasn't forthcoming, resorted to whiskey. Most guests understood that Elizabeth needed to be alone for part of the day, to get on with her work, and from Seán O'Faoláin we gain an inkling of just how exacting and exhausting that work was. He had blithely imagined a cascade of words and images flowing effortlessly from her pen; but once, when he burst into her study at Bowen's Court, 'She turned to me a forehead spotted with beads of perspiration.'

All the professional activity of the post-war years interfered with the Camerons' plan to spend more time in Ireland; but neither of them had relinquished the idea. In 1951 it became necessary to put the plan into action. Alan

Cameron suffered a heart attack, and was told by his doctor that he must stop work completely. He was greatly over-weight – even as far back as the early thirties, we remember, Virginia Woolf and others had remarked on his stoutness – and for many years he'd been a hard drinker. (A lot of people mention Elizabeth's drinking too but there is no sug-gestion that she ever became drunk; certainly it would have been out of keeping with her natural composure and self-control if she'd done so.) Now Alan's drinking started early in the morning.

Clarence Terrace was given up (the lease of the house being taken over by Louis MacNeice), and, after Christmas, the Camerons transferred themselves and their possessions to Bowen's Court. (Among the less charitable of their acquaintances the story circulated that Elizabeth whisked Alan off to Ireland to keep him out of sight.) They had eight months there before Alan died. In the last weeks of his life he was confined to bed, while Elizabeth, imperturbable as ever, coped with some (we imagine) not very welcome guests. These were the American poet and critic John Malcolm Brinnin (who includes a stinging account of the occasion in his book *Sextet*, published in 1982), and a friend of his called Robert. On the first night, while rooms were made ready for them, they had to put up at a hotel in Fermoy, where the chambermaid, early the next morning, treated them to a rendering of 'Mother Machree'.

From Brinnin, we gain an impression of Elizabeth talking authoritatively, caustically and non-stop, leaving her guests with no word of explanation whenever a cry of, *'Elizabeth!!!'*, was heard from upstairs (the piece is entitled *'Elizabeth!!!* A

Visit'), and returning to complete whatever statement she was making at the point of interruption. It's a new view of Elizabeth, one which credits her with extraordinary aplomb and outspokenness (showing her, for example, as being ready to pronounce on the shortcomings of her friends, such as their assumption that they may drop in on her whenever they choose), and contains no softening elements at all. Others refer to her kindness, sympthetic manner, unfailing courtesy, endearingness and so forth: but not Brinnin. Whatever his defects as a reporter, he isn't bland. Unfortunately, in some of the statements he attributes to Elizabeth, the facts are so wide of the mark that she can't possibly have uttered them. For example, he has her say: 'When I was a child, my mother and I, poor relations that we were then, were invited over to Bowen's Court.' Child of the house a poor relation! Talking about Virginia Woolf, too, she's supposed to have offered the information that Cyril Connolly 'once brought' her to Bowen's Court (we remember how Virginia Woolf reacted when she found the Connollys *in situ* during her one visit to the place).

Brinnin also has Elizabeth call Cyril Connolly a libertine, allude to the 'shameless curiosity' and voyeurism of Virginia Woolf – 'She wanted to know exactly who did what with whom and where, particularly if it was not in bed' – and remark on T. S. Eliot's reliance on alcohol as an aid to inspiration. In Charles Ritchie's diaries – one of our best sources of information about Elizabeth, as he would often jot down what she'd been saying, or record something about her that struck him – there's the following entry for 4 December 1941: 'Elizabeth says that T. S. Eliot told her that without alcohol he would never have got in the mood for his poems. That is good news!' It seems singularly odd that Elizabeth, eleven years on, should advert to this surely half-joking remark of Eliot's, and indeed engage in literary gossip at all, while her husband, between drink, dropsy, diabetes and a heart condition, lay dying upstairs. (Brinnin also notes the amount of alcohol 'put away' by Elizabeth herself: a number of whiskeys and soda, several glasses of champagne and several more of burgundy, before they sat down to nightcaps.) Was her rather peremptory, rather flashy performance on this occasion an effect of stress, combined with a stiff-necked determination to keep going?

Keep going she did, taking her American visitors on a trip to visit some neighbours, where they listened, without joining in, to some lofty and affected talk, and heard someone observe to their hostess, 'Darling, haven't you done something extraordinary to your hair?'

'"It's had a wash," said Elizabeth.'

Going on to London, Brinnin met the critic John Hayward (a frequent visitor to Clarence Terrace before the war) who, hearing of the Irish trip, immediately demanded to be told whether Elizabeth was 'still devoting body and soul to that hopeless old blimp?' Perhaps he hadn't forgiven Alan Cameron for something that had happened in the past. Hayward was a cripple, and on one occasion, when he'd come to call on Elizabeth, Alan offered to carry him down to his car. He got him safely out through the front door, but then dropped him in the gutter.

Alan died on 26 August 1952 and was buried in Farahy churchyard. Elizabeth, reluctant to face the coming winter alone at Bowen's Court, told her friend Veronica Wedgwood that she hoped to spend Christmas in the United States. She did, visiting New Jersey, Princeton, New York and Memphis, and no doubt making a detour to see Charles Ritchie (throughout their entire relationship, Victoria Glendinning says, they were never separated for more than a few months at a time). The positions of these two were now reversed: it was he who wasn't free to marry. He had married his cousin in 1948.

Veronica Wedgwood stayed at Bowen's Court in the winter of 1953 – an excellent guest, since she was working (on her book, *The King's Peace*) as hard as her hostess. (After Alan's death, Elizabeth embarked on a novel, *A World of Love*, which was published in 1955.) The visitor noted the splendid new curtains, of pink corset-satin, which had appeared in the drawing-room. The alterations planned by Elizabeth and Alan were still being carried out by Elizabeth. Although his death left her feeling maimed, as she wrote to someone similarly bereaved in 1966, she felt she owed it to him to make the effort to live her life well; this meant throwing herself with renewed vigour into work, travel, lecture tours, entertaining and so on.

In Rome, at one point, she bumped into John Lehmann, and urged him to come to Bowen's Court to finish the autobiography he was then writing. He did, and has recorded the visit in his book *The Ample Proposition* (1966). After working all morning, he says, Elizabeth would spend the afternoon in 'tireless, striding walks about the countryside, talking all the time'; or else set off in her car, driving 'like one possessed, mainly on the wrong side of the

road, for shopping or sight-seeing purposes'. Then it was
tea, dinner guests and friends.

He comments on her 'stylish, rather masculine carriage',
saying she looks as if she is 'about to settle on a shooting-
stick and lift binoculars', notes 'the old walled garden,
full of dahlias and fruit bushes', at Bowen's Court; and,
indoors, is 'particularly struck by one of the most beautiful
sofa-tables, in coromandel wood, I had ever seen'. He was
making plans for the projected *London Magazine* at the time,
and, in the course of discussing it with Elizabeth, clarified
his ideas about the sort of review he wanted it to be. Elizabeth, along with Veronica Wedgwood, Rex Warner, William
Plomer and John Hayward, was on the editorial board which
got together at a luncheon party some time later ('an
animated and stimulating occasion,' John Lehmann says).

John Malcolm Brinnin mentions his acquaintance with
certain young women, 'some of them famous, bold enough
to hint, or to boast', that their bids for attention from Elizabeth 'had not gone unheeded, neither in print nor in bed'.
What can he mean? The imputation of lesbian tendencies to
Elizabeth has very little to substantiate it. Like most other
people, she had female friends: that seems to be the gist of it.
We know that Nancy Spain was rebuffed, and not reinstated,
after once making a pass at Elizabeth. May Sarton, who fell
in love with her, was not left in any doubt about Elizabeth's
feelings for *her*: mild friendship, nothing more. May Sarton,
in the end, fell out of favour altogether, or felt that she had
done so. It was during her last visit to Bowen's Court, in the
mid 1950s, that her hostess (she says) made much of another guest, a young Californian woman, and left May out

in the cold. Perhaps May's manner simply left Elizabeth cold, at that particular moment – on other occasions, we remember, a like change of heart occurred. ('There is nothing like the variety of the neighbour or the new acquaintance,' Elizabeth wrote in an essay for *Contact*, 'nothing like the monotony of the intimate. To break new ground involves a fascinating discovery . . .')

A World of Love – dedicated to Catherine Collins, at whose home in New Jersey Elizabeth had got down to the book in the winter following Alan's death – is, from the title onward, the most openly romantic of the Bowen novels. It starts with a girl, Jane Danby, aged twenty, trailing in a summer haze across an early-morning field in Ireland, in an Edwardian dress. (This scene anticipates by a good many years the vogue for antique clothes.) The dress, white muslin, has come from a trunk in an attic, and so has the letter Jane is reading, a love letter, taken from a bundle held together with a rubber band – the rubber eroded. The author of the letters is a soldier dead since 1918, but to whom are they written? No superscription appears. The soldier, Guy, a cousin of Jane's father, and once the fiancé of her mother, has left his house, Montforte, to another cousin, Antonia, at whose instigation the Danbys are installed. Antonia, the worldly woman in the book, who turns up whenever she chooses, is staying at Montforte. This is the framework, over which trails the romantic idiom, embodied in Jane, like a clambering rose. Jane, we are told, is in a trance (the *bois dormant* motif again). She falls in love with a love letter; because of her, at a dinner party at a nearby castle, long-dead Guy all but materializes. As a focus for the emotions,

Guy has to do for her – until the very end of the book, when an instance of love at first sight occurs. All mood and no plot, you could say, with a very generalized theme: things rising up out of the past to overwhelm the present, which we've encountered before. It is, indeed, the book in which certain Bowen figments – the untried, expectant youthful state, the dead young soldier lover, complexities in the past, the house in Ireland – are savoured for their own sake, and not for the bearing they have on the course of events. All very lovely and effulgent, however: and it was Elizabeth's farewell to her lyrical manner.

The 1950s, Elizabeth told William Plomer, was the first decade in which she had 'enjoyed being grown-up as much as I expected to do when I was a child'. To this enjoyment, the trips to America, her Fellowship at Bryn Mawr, the doctorate conferred on her by Oxford University, a spell as writer in residence at the American Academy in Rome, a visit of Charles Ritchie's to Bowen's Court, old friends like the Cecils and Eddy Sackville-West (who bought a house in Ireland not far from Elizabeth's), new friends like Iris Murdoch and, in Ireland, Stephen and Lady Ursula Vernon, all contributed something. But, before the decade was out, a deeply distressing step had been forced on her. Frantic work, which she'd undertaken for the purpose, couldn't stave it off any longer. She had to sell Bowen's Court.

EIGHT

'My reasons for not more often coming to London are of the most banal kind: it's all so expensive,' Elizabeth wrote to William Plomer. Money mattered. One reason why she spent so much time in America was that more could be earned there. She didn't turn up her nose at articles like 'How to be Yourself but not Eccentric', or 'The Case for Summer Romance', when they were offered. This sort of thing paid well, if (as Victoria Glendinning says) not well enough. 'It was a losing battle.' It is hard to think of Elizabeth struggling with such topics, putting her proper work to one side and going all out to meet the demands of her ancestral home ('first Bowen house on the first Bowen's land'). In 1959, failure had to be faced; the house went on the market. Elizabeth, who'd consulted no one, accepted the first offer, from a Corkman named Cornelius O'Keefe. O'Keefe, she thought, would make it his home. Instead, he demolished it. By the end of 1960, the Farahy lands of Garrett Cushin were as bare as they'd been in Colonel Henry Bowen's day. Elizabeth, determinedly unrepining, wrote in her postscript to *Bowen's Court*: 'It was a clean end. Bowen's Court never lived to be a ruin.' However, Victoria Glendinning quotes Eddy Sackville-West's remark to Molly Keane, about the change in Elizabeth's appearance which struck him when he saw her soon after the sale: 'She looks like someone who has attended her own execution.'

Her travel book, *A Time in Rome*, came out in 1960, and caused Evelyn Waugh to count her out of the running in the literary stakes ('It has been a bad year for the old steeple-chasers'). Hermione Lee calls it 'fanciful and indulgent'. Perhaps, in this book, the Bowen imagination isn't functioning with its customary acuity; but *A Time in Rome* is none the less a perfectly creditable and interesting assembly of personal observations and impressions. Elizabeth is reading a detective novel on the first page when she arrives in Rome, having increasingly become an addict of that genre (detective stories, she said, are 'the only above-board grown-up children's stories'), and needing – with the Bowen's Court business very much on her mind – any available inducement to high spirits. (She had always enjoyed such authors as Agatha Christie, Nancy Spain and 'Nicholas Blake'; and later in the sixties, one of her neighbours at Hythe introduced her to the work of P. D. James, which she read with enormous relish.)

Back in England, and in need of somewhere to settle, Elizabeth started retracing her steps. First she took a flat at Old Headington, Oxford, in a house belonging to Isaiah Berlin, and within sight of her own old home, Waldencote. (While she was here, in 1962, another collection of her non-fiction pieces – a successor to the *Collected Impressions* of 1950 – *Afterthought*, was published.) Her next and final move was back to the Kentish town of Hythe, where she'd last lived with her mother at the age of twelve. There, she bought for herself an unattractive modern home: two-bedroom, red-brick. (One bedroom was assigned to Charles Ritchie, who came when he could.) She called it 'Carbery'. It's an unexpected final habitat for someone who had nearly always lived in pleasing surroundings – let alone a Bowen's Court Bowen. Still, she had a hill remembered from childhood outside her front door. Victoria Glendinning says Elizabeth 'loved' Carbery; it would have been more understandable if she'd taken it on in a mood of defiance and perversity.

The previous year (1964) Elizabeth's penultimate novel, *The Little Girls*, had come out. For this as well, she went back to the Kentish part of her childhood, though not in a mood of nostalgia: it was, as she told William Plomer, 'what the Americans would call "a recall of sensory experience" book'. We have a school, St Agatha's, in the summer of 1914, girls in butcher-blue dotted about the grounds, three more-or-less bosom friends, Dicey, Mumbo and Sheikie. It is Dicey who lives a little unconventionally with her charming mother; Mumbo (Clare) is rather gruff and clever; while Sheikie (Sheila), child of well-off parents, gets the sardonic tag: 'Southstone's wonder, the child exhibition dancer'. A box, containing secret items, is buried in the school grounds by these three, for 'posterity' to disinter. In the event, they disinter it themselves, to find nothing: a symbolic moment. The middle section of *The Little Girls*, in which these characters are eleven, is separated from the other two sections by more than fifty years – and as far as tone and atmosphere are concerned, it's by far the best part of the book. When we reach the present, with three old ladies vying with one another to be as bright, assertive and cryptic as possible, things are less satisfactory. The task the author set herself – to write a complex novel while allowing her characters to keep their thoughts to themselves – means that every statement and action has to be loaded; and some end up overloaded. Also, with this novel and its successor, *Eva Trout* (1969), it became apparent that Elizabeth was no longer as finely attuned to the spirit of the time as she had been. 'Her time', the time which her best work exemplifies, was in the past; as she wrote to William Plomer about his book *At Home*, it was 'the best account of your and my times, and of having such times as one's own times, that I know'.

She had written bravely, in the 1950s, of her belated enjoyment of the grown-up state; by the following decade, however, she wasn't merely grown-up, she was old. And old age was something to which she didn't take kindly. However, as she said in a television interview, the main thing, as far as she was concerned, was 'to keep the show on the road'. No one was going to catch her making a poor mouth. People who knew her in the Carbery era remember her as 'great fun', full of charm and ready for anything. She would leap into her motor car, at a moment's notice, to get together with an old friend. The famous hospitality continued, although now guests were put up at the White Hart Hotel in Hythe. A final volume of stories had come out the year she moved – *A Day in the Dark*, which brought together everything written in the post-war period. In the same year she started working on *Eva Trout*. 'This mannered manner

... was not quite the thing, no,' she has a character in the book say of a letter written by another character. 'Yet the ambiguities in themselves had one sort of merit, a sort of promise – one was at least on the verge of the Henry James country.' Here she is surely poking fun at herself, bearing in mind the standard criticism of her sometimes elaborate effects. *Eva Trout*, to be sure, suffers no diminution of liveliness; but the author has let her mannered manner run away with her. As an attempt to render a modern, nerve-ridden society, it goes even more awry than *The Little Girls*.

Eva Trout, who harks back to Valeria Cuffe in the 1930s story, 'Her Table Spread', is an ungainly orphan heiress, twenty-four at the start of the novel, and thirty-two on her later return from America, accompanied by the 'son' whom she has acquired illegally. She's an impossibly inflated version of the Bowen destructive innocent, and she meets an inflated end: shot dead by the other lethal innocent (her 'son') on Victoria Station. It's been said – with justice – that Elizabeth Bowen ended by parodying herself, trying to turn her old images and ideas to topical uses. However, we have *Pictures and Conversations* – or enough of it to make it an eternal cause of regret that she didn't complete the autobiography she was planning. Her three chapters – 'Origins', 'Places', and 'People' – were published posthumously, in 1974, in conjunction with other writings. 'If anybody *must* write a book about Elizabeth Bowen, why should not Elizabeth Bowen?' she'd asked, mildly fed up with commentators on her life and work who got things wrong. And what a book it would have been: illuminating, idiosyncratic and atmospheric. The underlying theme would have been the relationship 'between living and writing' (perhaps at its most interesting, she remarked characteristically, 'when it is apparently not traceable'). The fragment of this book that exists 'fairly ripples with life' (in Eudora Welty's phrase).

Pictures and Conversations (the title taken from *Alice's Adventures in Wonderland*) was begun the year *Eva Trout* was published in England, 1969. Elizabeth must already have been suffering from the lung cancer that killed her; but she still managed to get about, teaching for a term at Princeton that year, and attending the usual parties and other social gatherings. A new departure for her was a small children's book, called *The Good Tiger*, and another was the Nativity play she wrote in 1970, which was put on that Christmas in the Protestant Cathedral in Derry: a hopeful gesture, at that time, since it brought large numbers of Protestants and Catholics together in the audience. (The writer Hubert Butler, a cousin of Elizabeth's, alludes in one of his essays to the bitterness she'd come to feel about Ireland, and expressed to him shortly before her death: and says he hopes that illness was responsible for her state of mind, and not utter disillusionment. But the disintegration in the north must have troubled her, running, counter, as it did to every principle she cherished: order, stability, tolerance, good will, a civilized outlook.)

1971 was not a good year for Elizabeth. To her chronic smoker's cough, and chronic bronchitis, were added pneumonia and a septic foot (she'd stabbed it with a pruning tool, and it didn't heal). Still she struggled over to Ireland (Victoria Glendinning tells us) to stay with her friends the Vernons, in 'one shoe and one silver slipper'. In 1972 she was still driving about in her dirty, smoky car, and keeping up a stream of talk even when she was inside the car and out of earshot. She never stopped talking. Stephen Spender (in his *Journals 1939–1983*) remembers driving Elizabeth back from Oxford on one occasion, and straining to follow her non-stop monologue, but being able to catch only a word here and there – a lifetime's smoking having affected her vocal powers. 'I had a sense of unreality, as though the car I was driving was a crayon or chalk making a line across a landscape of paper.' Eventually, her voice gave out altogether: it was at this point that Charles Ritchie, flying straight over from Canada, made her see a specialist. She was whisked into hospital, where she carried out her duties as a Booker Prize judge. A course of radium treatment followed in the summer, and she believed the illness was being defeated. She could only whisper.

Christmas came, and her usual trip to Ireland, where she shocked everyone by the awfulness of her appearance. In the new year, back in Hythe, she found it impossible to manage any longer. She went into hospital again. Visitors flocked to see her; then she was too ill for all but her oldest friends. Her cousin Audrey Fiennes and Charles Ritchie came every day. Spencer Curtis Brown, her literary executor, came and noted her instruction regarding the outline for an autobiography: 'I want it published,' she said. Then she was left alone with her cousin, and then with Charles Ritchie. Early in the morning, on 22 February 1973, she died. She was buried in Ireland, in Farahy churchyard, just inside the old Bowen's Court gates on the road between Mitchelstown and Mallow. She had, throughout her life, what she once called 'an artist's impulse and wish for everyone to live at full height'; and, as her friend Eudora Welty said, 'She was a prime responder to this world.'

INDEX

INDEX